The Orvis® Guide to
FAMILY FRIENDLY
FLY FISHING

Tom Rosenbauer

LYONS PRESS
Guilford, Connecticut
An imprint of Globe Pequot Press

Lyons Press is an imprint of Globe Pequot Press.

Photos by Tom Rosenbauer unless otherwise noted.
Illustrations on pages 87 and 89 by Peter Chadwell © Morris Book Publishing, LLC

Project editor: Meredith Dias
Text design and layout: Sue Murray

Library of Congress Cataloging-in-Publication Data

Rosenbauer, Tom.
 The Orvis guide to family friendly fly fishing / Tom Rosenbauer.
     p. cm.
 Includes index.
 ISBN 978-0-7627-7908-6
 1. Fly fishing. I. Title.
 SH456.R667 2013
 799.12'4—dc23

2012018716

Printed in the United States of America

10 9 8 7 6 5 4 3 2 1

Contents

Introduction

Fly fishing was not an institution in my family. In fact, as hard as I try to imagine it, I can't see my mother, father, and sister joining me on a fly-fishing trip. It's too bizarre an image to even speculate on the results. No, when the family went on vacation to Nova Scotia or Maine or the Adirondacks, I'd be the geeky teenager with the fly rod chasing brook trout with wet flies and gawking at the salmon the adult anglers caught, while the rest of my family waited not-so-patiently on the bank.

I did see my father fish with a fly rod twice. The first time, he took me to a spring creek that he read about in the paper that was supposedly teeming with trout. It was a crowded public stretch with no wading allowed, and my father dug up a steel fly rod and automatic reel from the depths of the garage and let me go along to watch. I stood on the bank in awe while he yelled "Stand back!" to anyone within earshot and flailed the line around in the air. He gave up after a half hour, and it was many years until I saw him with a fly rod again.

My father was not a patient man. He did not have the time I did as an eleven-year-old to practice on the lawn for hours on end and explore local sunfish ponds, preparing for the trout streams in my future. My one driving lesson with him lasted exactly three minutes, after he yelled that I was at the controls of a two-ton machine and was about to kill both of us. And even later in life, when I suggested he attend a fly-fishing school so that we could fish together, he was too proud to take lessons. Children of the Depression were not as open to learning adult skills by paying someone to teach them.

The last time I saw my father with a fly rod in his hands was in exactly the same place I saw him the first time—on the banks of that spring creek. He was progressing rapidly beyond the middle stages of Alzheimer's and I wanted to do a father-and-son thing with him before it was too late. So I took him fishing, and by this time, thirty years later, I had become intimately familiar with that spring creek.

I set him up on a lower stretch, tying on a nymph and a strike indicator, figuring that he could manage that all right and wouldn't get into any trouble. I started upstream, saw a few rises around the bend, and attempted to crack the code of several trout rising to very tiny insects. I got lost in my fishing, something I frequently do, and when I glanced at my watch, thirty minutes had gone by and I had not seen my father because I had slipped around the bend. Some son I was, leaving a father with dementia all alone on the banks of a trout stream. When I got to him, he was in exactly the same place, watching his strike indicator dangling in the current, perfectly content, with an uncharacteristically serene composure. It's a bittersweet memory I treasure. We finally got to fly fish together, and it made him happy.

I'm now teaching my wife, Robin, and seven-year-old son, Brett, fly fishing (actually I followed my own advice and sent Robin off to school to learn how to cast). Robin seems to enjoy it; I'm uncertain about Brett. He loves bugs and reptiles and creatures of all sorts, but he doesn't exactly bug me to go fishing, and I don't want to force him, so the jury is still out on whether he will be a future fly-fishing buddy.

That's always the risk of sharing your passion with the rest of the family. It seldom turns out the way you daydream about it. But hopefully with the advice in this book, you and your family will at least be able to enjoy some aspects of this fascinating pastime together. Whether you're an experienced fly fisher looking for tips on intriguing and teaching your family, or a novice yourself hoping to learn along with them, I think you'll pick up some valuable tips here. Many talented and experienced people helped me gather information for these chapters, so you're benefitting from a large pool of empirical results.

I wish you the best of luck, and always remember that it's just fishing, and that fly fishing is supposed to refresh rather than frustrate.

Chapter 1

What's So Great about Fly Fishing?

In 1973 I was taking an undergraduate ornithology class at the New York State College of Environmental Science and Forestry, and the study skin on the table in front of the class had me drooling with desire.

No matter how different their backgrounds, fly fishers usually become instant friends because of their shared passion.

We were examining the skin of a drake wood duck. The feathers from the flank of a male wood duck are highly prized by fly tiers, and in the 1970s wood duck populations were at a low level and the feathers were thus expensive and hard to find. As one of the other students picked up the skin to examine it, a perfect flank feather separated from the skin and drifted to the floor. My hand snapped out to catch it, but before I could bend over to actually grab it, another hand, quicker than mine and closer to the feather's wobbling descent, snatched it from the air. Half bent over in my attempt to grab the feather, I looked up into the triumphant eyes of our teaching assistant, a graduate student in fisheries biology named Terry Finger.

"Fly tier?" he asked.

"Yup. You?"

"Born and raised near the Esopus, trained by Ray Smith."

The Esopus is a famous Catskill trout stream, and Ray Smith was a cantankerous old local known throughout the world of fly fishing as one of the finest fly tiers in the region. Terry and I became fast friends simply based on that single fleeting moment, and we became fishing buddies, exploring trout streams like the Beaverkill in the Catskills, the Battenkill in Vermont, and a number of secret meadow streams in upstate New York. We stayed in touch during his PhD studies in Oregon and later when he moved to Missouri to work in fisheries management. He died tragically of a heart attack while hiking in his beloved Catskills while home for a visit, and I still miss his soft laugh over long-distance phone lines.

Fly fishers, in chance meetings at social functions like school conferences or weddings or soccer games, invariably gravitate to each other, get locked in conversation, and often tune out the rest of the world until they are yanked apart by long-suffering spouses or the sounds of the "Wedding March." It can become more than a sport, more than a hobby, and at best the obsession brings individuals from all walks of life together in a strong bond. Approached and taught properly, imagine what a passion that turns strangers into instant friends can do for a family.

Fly Fishing Is Satisfying on Many Levels

Although fly fishing is just another form of fishing, its approach to catching fish gives it some features that distinguish it from bait or spin fishing. With bait fishing, on the end of your line is something alive (or recently alive) that is attractive to fish by virtue of its movement, appearance, and smell. Fish will find your bait—you can sit back, enjoy the weather, daydream, and even listen to music, read, or eat lunch while you wait for the fish to bite. Spin or bait casting with an artificial lure is more active in that you can and often have to cover a large expanse of water by casting and retrieving your lure over as wide an area as possible to find willing fish.

With a fly rod you have neither the smell nor movement of live bait, nor the ability to cover as wide an area as you can with an artificial lure. Fly fishing therefore requires more hunting, more stalking, because the fly must be placed near a hungry fish and then manipulated by the angler to make it look realistic. Sometimes the current does the work for you, but even if you are using the current to make your offering look like a real insect or baitfish, you have to constantly manipulate the fly line to make sure the current moves the fly in a lifelike manner.

So when actively fly fishing, you have little downtime. No reading books. No listening to music (you might miss the sound of a fish feeding). No daydreaming. Your mind is constantly focused on the task at hand, which is what makes fly fishing appealing to many people. You *can't* worry about the mortgage payment or the result of that memo you wrote yesterday. You get totally immersed in the task at hand: mentally, physically, and emotionally.

Fly fishers often get so immersed in the quest that they develop tunnel vision. I was once steelhead fishing in British Columbia, filming an episode of a TV show, and even though the camera was on me and I was surrounded by spectacular scenery, I got into my own little world, trying to will a steelhead to swim through the pool and take my fly. Although I had no idea if there were any steelhead within a mile of me, I kept thinking that maybe if I changed the swing of my fly just a bit, I could enchant

These guys are so intent on getting to a fishing spot that they may not notice the natural beauty around them.

a lone steelhead into smacking the fly aside with its jaws. When I got back to shore, the cameraman said, "Did you see the bear?"

"What bear?" I asked

"The bear about 30 feet from you on the far bank."

Apparently a black bear had wandered down the bank, poked around in some bushes, looked at me with curiosity, and ambled off when it realized I was not very interesting. I had been so engrossed in the fishing, I was totally oblivious.

The Clinical Value of Fly Fishing

There is a wealth of anecdotal and semiprofessional evidence connected with the use of fly fishing as therapy for chronic illness and injury. The immensely popular Casting for Recovery organization, where survivors of breast cancer get together on fly-fishing outings in a wellness rather than an illness setting, has been described by many of the participants as "life changing." The motion of fly fishing provides valuable physical therapy; the ability to solve problems takes the women far away from their daily struggles; and the kinship shared by a group with a shared passion has proven to be a successful formula.

A more clinical result was related to me by counseling psychologist Greg Burchstead. In a study of Iraq War veterans with missing limbs who were also suffering from post-traumatic stress disorder, conducted by researchers from the University of Southern Maine, the University of Utah, and the Salt Lake City Veterans Administration, levels of cortisol, formed by the degradation of epinephrine and associated with high levels of stress without a consequent reduction of the stress, were measured two weeks before a weekend of fly fishing and immediately after the weekend event, followed by an evaluation six weeks later. Cortisol levels were significantly reduced immediately after the fishing trip and were still at a lower level than the initial measurement six weeks later.

Just as noteworthy were statistically valid improvements in sleep patterns, lower levels of depression and anxiety, significant and sustained reductions in somatic stress (faintness, chest pains, nausea), and significant and sustained reductions in guilt, hostility, fear, and sadness. And finally the most positive result of the study was that three months later, 50 percent of the participants were still fly fishing, continuing to reap its benefits.

For years I've looked for a landmark psychological study that proved beyond a shadow of a doubt the value of fly fishing to individuals and families. Ultimately I realized I was looking for clinical, peer-reviewed proof of something that is so patently obvious, such proof probably does not exist. Imagine going to a psychologist and asking, "Do you think an outdoor activity that I can do with my whole family, which incorporates some elements of problem solving, an appreciation of nature, and moderate physical activity, would be beneficial?" And the psychologist's professional answer, "D'ya think? Any more questions?" Followed by a bill for several hundred dollars.

Fly Fishing Is Great for What Ails You

Fly fishing is healthy for your brain, but it is also not bad for your body. The image most people have of fishing is sitting in a boat or on a dock waiting for a fish to swim by and take your bait. However, in fly fishing you are almost always moving, particularly if you are wading. You're hunting and stalking fish because a fly doesn't cover much territory—you must find the fish and only then do you begin fishing. So whether you are wading a small mountain stream for trout, walking along saltwater grass beds for redfish, or chasing schools of striped bass down a long sandy beach, you can get your heart pumping.

When I hit my mid-fifties, both my lifestyle and my metabolism slowed down with the inevitable thickening of my middle region. My wife, who is much more disciplined about fitness than I am, was using a heart monitor to measure how many calories she burned, and when I got serious about losing fifteen pounds, I figured I would try one. I dutifully wore the monitor through the winter, pounding away on an elliptical machine every day, watching the pounds ebb. Never a fan of gyms or indoor exercise of any kind, I decided to begin measuring the calories I burned while I was fishing.

I have a little mountain brook trout stream that I often fish on my lunch hour, so one day before I began fishing I strapped on the heart monitor. To my surprise and delight, I found that while wading this little stream, climbing over rocks and fighting the current, I could burn as many calories in the same amount of time as I could on the elliptical. Using the heart monitor on a bonefish trip to Belize later that year, I found that a few hours kayaking and wading the bonefish flats during the day allowed me to eat like a pig that night just to get enough calories into my body to prevent it from going into starvation mode.

So the next time you and your family head out for the local gym to breathe the stale air and watch your neighbors sweat and grunt, think instead about spending a few hours walking a local lakeshore, wading a stream, or taking a canoe or kayak onto a nearby pond. Your body *and* your mind will be renewed.

Fly Fishing Can Be Enjoyed by Anyone

The moderate but sustained physical activity associated with fly fishing makes it ideal for people of all ages. Although it requires moderate hand-eye coordination, most fly fishing does not call for the strength that other activities such as running, tennis, or contact sports require. Children can cast adult-size fly rods with ease, and unless elderly fly fishers develop arthritic conditions in their shoulders or arms, they can participate well into their later years. I know of many active fly fishers who are well into their eighties. A few years ago I spent a week with author/novelist/naturalist Peter Matthiessen, traveling by helicopter into Patagonia along coastal Chile for a week, and at eighty-three he was in and out of helicopters and fishing alongside much younger people for eight hours a day. My old boss, Leigh Perkins, retired CEO of the Orvis Company, still fly fishes (and hunts upland birds) over 300 days per year at age eighty-four. Don Puterbaugh, a guide on the Arkansas River in Colorado, at age eighty-two is still guiding fly fishers seventy-five to a hundred days a year.

Well into his eighties, writer and naturalist Peter Matthiessen still enjoys fly fishing, even when wading powerful rivers.

Some fly fishing is not for the very young or elderly. It can get as physically demanding as the participant wishes. Fly fishing for 100-pound bluefin tuna, playing 180-pound tarpon, or wading a raging steelhead river requires an angler in top physical shape. But that is what makes fly fishing so appealing, as it can deliver an adrenaline rush to the young hotshots, but they can still enjoy it in their later years by scaling down their trips to fly fishing on more gentle waters, where the mental stimulation is still challenging but the physical requirements are modest.

Fly Fishing Provides a Strong Connection to the Natural World

Our lives are increasingly distanced not only from the source of our food, but from the natural world in general. For many of us a connection with the natural world for any reason has become a distant memory overshadowed by work, school and community functions, and supposed "outdoor" activities like running or bicycling that get us outdoors but whiz us past the wonders of nature that delighted us when we were younger.

Even children are not immune, and most kids today suffer from what author Richard Louv, in his book *Last Child in the Woods,* calls nature-deficit disorder. His premise is that today's children have less access to the free play in the outdoors than children of past generations enjoyed. It's easy to blame the siren song of mentally stimulating computer games, but even our children's time outdoors is restricted to organized sports where virtually every move they make is directed by an adult. The result, according to Louv, is an increase in childhood ADHD, obesity, diabetes, and depression—all of which can be ameliorated by more free play in the outdoors.

Fly fishing provides a perfect foil to nature-deficit disorder in both children and adults. There is nothing less predictable than fishing. Every day is different. Changes in fish migration, food supply, weather conditions, and even the phase of the moon affect where fish will be and when they will feed. It's this very unpredictability that makes fishing so appealing: We are forced to think and improvise constantly, but

Flies, and the critters they imitate, are fascinating to people of all ages.

always with the knowledge that it is nature that makes the rules, and the rules change hourly.

Fishing with flies adds another level of natural interaction because, in much of fly fishing, we strive to imitate exactly what fish feed upon, which calls for yet another level of understanding and study. Not only do we need to connect with our quarry the fish, and understand their natural history and behavior, we also should understand the life cycle and behavior of their prey. This does not mean that a fly fisher needs a degree in ichthyology or entomology. In much of fly fishing, the need to study a fish's prey is overemphasized, and many effective flies are just fanciful creations that imitate nothing in nature. But the door to learn more is always open.

Fly Fishing Myths and Misconceptions

Although fly fishing is simply another way to impale a hook into a fish's mouth, there are many popular notions about it that should be dispelled.

It's Too Expensive.

Because spinning and bait-casting rods can be bought in a big-box store for under $30, and because a middle-of-the-road fly rod costs around $250 and the cheapest you can go is about $50, it seems like fly fishing is much more expensive than spin fishing or bait casting. But we ask a lot more of a fly rod. We use it to cast the line over and over, sometimes needing to keep the line in the air, under control, for multiple casts. We use a fly rod to reposition line on the water, and finally to play a fish. And if you look at the offerings in any of the big general tackle catalogs, you'll see as many spin rods offered at $250 and up as you do models for less than $30. Do you really think the guy with the $50,000 bass boat is using a $30 rod?

When I take my son to the lake to fish for sunfish with worms, I can buy everything I need for twenty bucks at the general store down the street. Because spin rods and push-button spin-casting rods are more mainstream, though, many more inexpensive options are available because the cost of producing kids' outfits in huge quantities brings the price way down. The cost of entry *is* higher for fly fishing. If I wanted to take my son fly fishing for those same sunfish, I'd have to spend around $50 for a rod, $30 for a reel, $30 for a line, plus a few bucks for a leader and a few flies. So the basic price is higher, but it's about the same as an iPod or a portable game player—and it won't be obsolete next year.

It is also true that you can spend a few thousand dollars on a high-end fly rod, reel, and line, plus premium waders, a bunch of gadgets, and a good selection of flies. But you can also spend the same amount for a spin-fishing outfit, and some spinning lures cost more than $25 each!

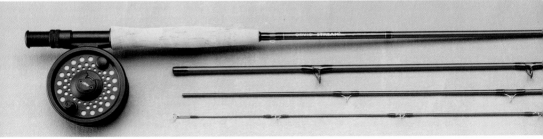

Fly fishing is not prohibitively expensive. This is a high-quality rod, reel, and line outfit, and it sells for under $200.

It's Just for Old Guys.

Twenty years ago this was a pretty safe statement. For some strange reason, I decided I wanted to try fly fishing when I was about eleven years old, and I taught myself as much as I could throughout my teenage years. I attended the local Trout Unlimited meetings regularly, where I was by far the youngest member, almost like a mascot, and all my fishing buddies except one were at least twenty years older than me. When I went to college I was the only fly fisherman in my fraternity house; in fact, the guys I lived with had not a clue about fly fishing, except that the fly-tying materials on my desk were something to play with when they were stoned.

Then in 1992 a movie was released called *A River Runs Through It,* based on the novel by Norman Maclean and lovingly produced by Robert Redford. The grumpy old guys who had practiced their dark art in relative obscurity were suddenly joined by brash, enthusiastic youngsters who, admittedly, did not always appreciate the history, traditions, and streamside ethics of the old guard. Trout streams got crowded. Grumbling about yuppies was rampant. Range Rovers were parked alongside old Jeeps at popular fishing access sites. It was a zoo at first, but those who really didn't have the patience for the finer points of fly fishing soon moved on to the next big thing, and the fly-fishing world, swelled slightly but still a tiny niche, settled down.

The one permanent effect of "The Movie" was the entrance of more young people into this tiny world. Suddenly college kids were getting interested in fly fishing in a way I had never seen before in my forty years observing this business. They learned casting from YouTube, traded stories on blogs, and studied podcasts and Internet radio shows. They made movies in the tradition of the Warren Miller ski movies and later snowboard films. Fly-fishing photography morphed from mostly quiet studies of lone anglers smoking pipes and gazing longingly at distant mountains to edgy angle-cropped shots, extreme wide angles from low perspectives, and artsy sepia-toned photos with intentional grain or noise.

Few young people will admit to being inspired by *A River Runs Through It* because it would be embarrassing for most to confess to being

Dusty Revel is a very serious fly fisher from northern California, and one look at his vehicle proves it. He is proof that the old pipe-smoking fly-fishing guy is a worn-out cliché.

lured into anything by Hollywood. However, I have a number of fishing buddies under thirty who, when pressed, will disclose that it was an inspiration to them, and that it was their first exposure to fly fishing and made a lasting impression.

With a few notable exceptions, fly fishing was historically a male-dominated sport. As late as the 1970s, Louise Miller, wife of the famous fly-fishing writer Alfred Miller (better known by his pen name Sparse Grey Hackle) and a fine angler herself, had to sit on the steps of the prestigious DeBruce Club on the upper Willowemoc in the Catskills while her husband and his cronies held court, smoked cigars, and drank scotch. Although you still see more men than women fly fishing today, you can hardly say it is an exclusive male domain anymore, and it is not just women accompanying their husbands or boyfriends. There are many highly qualified female guides in fly fishing today, and they row drift boats and run flats skiffs as hard as their male counterparts. In general, women do have different goals and expectations when fly fishing than men, which we'll explore in more detail in chapter 6.

All That Gear Makes It Too Complicated.

The vision of a fly fisher as seen in outdoor (and sometimes fashion) magazines is a person dressed in bulky waders, wearing a vest with about twenty pockets and all of them filled with mysterious items that must be acquired for success. The vest is adorned with multiple tiny retractors from which hang gadgets that look like they were filched from a dentist's office. When my wife, Robin, took her first fly-fishing class, her initial impression was, "I love the casting and trying to master that, but I was really intimidated by all the equipment you need to learn about. Just give me a few flies that will work and let me go off and fish."

There's no doubt that fly fishers can and do accumulate a lot of gear, but the complexity of the gear is part of the appeal to some. When you can catch anything from a small trout in a mountain stream to a sailfish in the Gulf Stream, it's natural that different gear will be required, and in the typical well-stocked fly shop, the owner never knows what the next person in the door will need. It's hard to make a living in a specialty fly shop, so the owner hedges his or her bets to make sure a sale is not lost.

Fly fishing can be really simple. For instance, for fishing a small pond for bass or sunfish, or a small meadow trout stream, this is all you really need:

- A rod, reel, line, and leader (what is commonly called a "fly-fishing outfit")

- Something to cut the leader after tying on a fly. It can be a special pair of fly fisherman's snips or the sharp scissors on your Swiss army knife, or even a pair of nail clippers.

- A spool or two of extra leader material, called "tippet" in fly fishing

- A box of flies. You can put a few in an old pill container or the free little plastic container they gave you when you bought the flies.

- A hat and sunglasses for sun and eye protection. You would need these no matter what you were doing outdoors anyway.

Fly fishing, and the gear you use, does not have to be very complicated to have a great day fishing.

You can wade in the water with a pair of sandals and shorts. If the water is cold, you may need a pair of waders, and if the bottom is slippery, you might need special wading shoes to keep your footing. But all the other gear can come later, if you wish. Keep it simple if, like Robin, you're intimidated by all that stuff.

It's Really Hard to Learn.

If you have sufficient coordination to drive a car, you can learn fly fishing. It requires minimal hand-eye coordination and almost no strength. A four-year-old can be taught to cast a fly rod in about ten minutes. Adults take a little longer because they have habits from other sports and activities that need to be unlearned. It's slightly harder to learn fly casting than spin fishing, as the cast is more dynamic and needs to stay under control to avoid getting the fly caught in trees or in the ground behind you. And manipulation of the fly requires more input from the angler—it's less mechanical than fishing with a conventional rod and reel, where you cast a lure or bait out and then reel it back with a mechanical device. In fly fishing the lure is retrieved by pulling line through your fingers, so although additional control is required, it's that sense of being in more control that adds to its satisfaction.

People who have grown up fly fishing find spin fishing difficult too. I was making a video about fly fishing one summer and was using nine-year-old Patrick Timmins as a model. Patrick grew up fly fishing in Colorado with his dad, and in one scene, where we wanted to compare fly fishing to spin fishing, we needed young Patrick to first cast a fly into a riffle and then cast a worm and bobber into the same piece of water. Patrick nailed the fly-casting part of it on the first take. He had never used a spinning rod, though, and after about a dozen casts where he either forgot to open the bail or didn't take his finger off the line, we had to fake the scene: I ran in and cast the spin outfit into the riffle, then quickly ducked out of the scene after handing the rod to Patrick. Most kids begin on a spin rod or push-button rod and then learn fly fishing later. Patrick just started the other way around, but had no less difficulty adjusting.

Patrick Timmins Jr., here with his dad, Patrick Timmins Sr., is a rare kid—he never fished with a spinning rod before learning to use a fly rod.

You Have to Learn Entomology to Get Good at It.

Although fly fishing is a wonderful way to catch trout and seems to be tailor-made for catching fish that feed on small insects, it is so much more. Today's flies imitate baitfish, leeches, crabs, shrimp, squids, frogs, and mice as well as insects. And while it's true that a little education on the different kinds of bugs that inhabit a trout stream can make trout fishing with a fly rod more productive, you need no entomology to happily catch trout for the rest of your life. Many fly fishers delve into the depths of entomology because they find it fascinating. They love and embrace the complexity of the relationship between aquatic insects and trout. But you don't need it to have fun, any more than you need to study advanced geometry to play billiards.

Fly Fishers Are Snobs.

You'll get no argument from me that *some* fly fishers are snobs and seem to think that fly fishing is somehow more pure or more "sporting" than other kinds of fishing. True, you don't have to get your hands dirty putting a worm or live minnow on a hook, but hands also stay clean when fishing spinner baits for bass or plugs for tarpon.

More sporting? Maybe. At times we do artificially tie one hand behind our backs when fly fishing, when a piece of live bait or even a spin lure would be a quicker way to catch fish. Then you hear the cliché about "getting a more sporting fight with that skinny little rod." But a fly rod, with its ability to protect a leader with its shock-absorbing qualities, can be a deadly efficient, fight-beating tool. Experienced fly-rod tarpon anglers regularly get 150-pound tarpon to the boat in half the time it would take on a spinning rod by using a 60-pound-test leader and utilizing the shock-absorbing qualities of a heavy fly rod to put constant pressure on a fish right from the start of the battle and never letting up.

The other argument from fly fishers who claim to be more pure is that fly fishing is mostly catch-and-release and that fish caught with a fly survive better than fish caught with conventional tackle. Time and time again scientific studies have shown that the difference in mortality rates between fish caught with flies and fish caught with spinning lures is negligible. Even fish caught with live bait and released survive far more often than is commonly thought.

Since the 1990s fly fishing has become much more of a populist sport enjoyed by people of all ages, from all walks of life. You'll run into the snobs here and there but they're easy to ignore, because for every snob you meet, there are a half-dozen other fly fishers who delight in sharing their knowledge with you.

Chapter 2

Introducing the Novice
to Fly Fishing

Fly fishing is just another way of sticking a hook in a fish's mouth, and although there remains the perception that it is a kind of cultish art, it's just fishing. In order to learn and understand fly fishing, I believe it's necessary to have a background in some other kind of fishing, what is often called "conventional" fishing. By that I mean fishing for sunfish with a worm and bobber on a push-button rod, or fishing for striped bass with a spinning rod and a plastic plug.

If you have not fished with conventional tackle, I urge you to go out and fish with bait before you try fly fishing. And if you plan on teaching a family member, I think a better foundation is developed by first taking him or her fishing with a worm and bobber. This is especially important for kids, but almost as important for adults. They have to get excited about their prey, feel the electric thrill when a fish is on the end of the line, and practice landing and releasing (or cleaning and eating) fish without other distractions. And although the concept of fly fishing is simple, there are a few more complexities involved, and they are easier to understand with a background in another kind of fishing.

A Proven Method

What follows is an almost fail-safe way of helping a novice fly fisher understand the principles of fly fishing in a real-world manner, without resorting to discussions of casting loops and leader-tippet relationships.

For someone who has never fished at all, a push-button rod should be the first step.

If you have never fished with a fly rod, you can follow this plan of action for yourself, but it works best when introducing a newcomer to fly fishing. You'll need, of course, a fly rod. Any old fly rod with a fly line that matches the rod will do. A reel should be attached to the rod, but for this exercise, and really for most of the fly fishing you and your family will do, the reel is just a line storage device.

Take one leader. A 7½-foot leader with a 2X or 3X tippet size is perfect. Don't worry about what the specifications mean; it's a tapered leader 7½ feet long with a breaking strength at the thin end of about 8 to 12 pounds.

You will also need a conventional rod and reel. I use a kid's push-button outfit that you can buy at a big-box store for less than $15. They typically come with a few bait hooks and a bobber, which you'll also need. However, any lightweight spinning or spin-casting outfit will work. For this experience you'll want 6-, 8-, or 10-pound-test line on the reel, which is what most inexpensive push-button outfits come with. It also helps to have a pair of forceps or needle-nose pliers to remove the hook from the fish and flatten the barb of the hook. When bait fishing, fish often take the bait deep into their throat, and the barbless hook makes it easy to remove, be it from a fish, an article of clothing—or human skin!

Next you need to find a pond, open lakeshore, saltwater estuary, or sheltered ocean cove. If you can find a dock or jetty, that's better yet, because your pupil will have an easier time watching the fish. Do a little research and find a place with abundant small fish that will eagerly take bait or a lure. In freshwater, sunfish like bluegills, pumpkinseeds, longears, rock bass, and shellcrackers are found close to shore most of the year and are always eager to bite. Small bass, either largemouth or smallmouth, are also worthwhile, but make sure your students understand that they will likely be below the legal size limit and must be released. Creek chubs and fallfish are large minnows that inhabit slow-moving streams in the East, and they are also eager biters. In the Rocky Mountains, whitefish inhabit slower, deeper currents in most rivers and respond eagerly to any small nymph. In salt water, find a place with an abundance of "schoolie" striped bass or "snapper" bluefish along the northern Atlantic; small redfish, sea

This is really all you need to go fly fishing: a rod, reel, and line outfit; a leader; and a few flies.

trout, or ladyfish in the southern Atlantic and Gulf coasts; or surf perch on the Pacific coast.

For the business end of the outfit, you will need some bait. Worms are fine, and almost any fish will take worms. If you plan on fishing in a saltwater pond or off a dock in the ocean, pick up some clam worms or similar bait. If it's grasshopper season, this exercise also works terrific with live grasshoppers in freshwater, as you'll see shortly. You will also need a few flies. They should be simple flies that match the kind of fish you'll be chasing. Here are some suggestions:

> **For the various sunfish and small freshwater bass:** Bluegill Bug size 12, grasshopper imitation (there are many to choose from and all work well) size 12, Bluegill Spider size 10, San Juan Worm size 10, Hare's Ear Nymph size 10

> **For small saltwater species:** Woolly Bugger size 8, Clouser Minnow size 6, Crazy Charlie size 6

You'll probably only need one of these patterns, but make sure you have at least three or four flies because you will lose some. It's part of the game. Don't worry about color options—pick the brightest one so your student can see it in the water. These fish won't care.

Step 1: Catch a Fish with Bait

Hopefully you've found a spot with clear water that is teeming with fish too small for most "serious" anglers to worry about. It might help to chum the water before fishing. Throw a few worms off the dock. If you've been able to catch some live grasshoppers (it's best to do this early in the morning, when the air is cool, because the cold-blooded insects can't move very fast until the sun heats them up), throw a few in the water and have your student watch the fish rise up and inhale them. Sunfish around docks are often fed bread by people pinching corners off their sandwiches, so try a few pinches of soft bread or canned corn. In salt water, a handful of chopped shrimp could not only bring the fish in closer, but will show your student how the fish feed.

Next put a piece of your chosen bait on the hook, and put a bobber about 2 feet above the bait. Stress to your student that the piece of bait won't go very far without the bobber, and although we use the bobber

The handsome pumpkinseed sunfish is always eager to take a fly or bait.

Get fish on the line quickly by beginning with bait and a bobber.

to tell when a fish has taken the bait, we also need its weight to pull line off the reel when we make a cast. If you've chosen your spot right, that's all the bobber will have to do because you'll be able to watch the fish take the bait. Elevation from a dock or jetty makes the fish easier to spot, as do sunglasses with polarized lenses that cut through the glare on the water's surface. And for safety's sake, anglers should always wear either sunglasses or prescription glasses to protect their eyes from airborne hooks. This is especially important with fly fishing.

If all goes well you'll catch a fish or, better yet, your student will catch a fish. Make sure they understand that because the bait smelled, felt, and tasted like natural food, the fish first attacked the bait, then held onto it and tried to swallow it. Show your student how to land the fish properly by reeling the bobber to within a foot of the rod tip, then swinging the rod around or up until you can grab the fish. Many of these fish have spiny dorsal fins, so show your student how to cradle the fish by pushing the dorsal spines down and holding them in place. Even small bluefish and sea trout have sharp teeth, so get those forceps or pliers ready to

You can use a fly on conventional tackle, and it's a good second step after using bait.

remove the hook. Have your student cradle the fish gently in the water until it regains its equilibrium, and then release the fish when it can swim away under its own power.

If you're having fun catching fish on bait and want to repeat the process, go ahead, especially when fishing with kids. But in any given spot, the fish do get wise to you after a few get removed from the water and most of them have seen your bait. If you really want to make this a fly-fishing lesson, hold off on catching too many with bait, before the fish get wise to the game.

Step 2: Catch a Fish on a Fly

Now explain to your student that you're going to try an artificial fly. This is why the grasshopper mode works so well, because you can go right from a live grasshopper to a fake one, making the transition to a fly so much more logical. If you want to make the same logical shift with a worm, try using a San Juan Worm for your artificial—although I find that a floating fly like a Bluegill Bug is more fun.

Cut the bait hook from your line and attach your chosen fly to the end of the line. Don't remove the bobber. Explain to your student that the tiny artificial fly weighs almost nothing, and if you tried to cast it by itself it wouldn't go anywhere because there is not enough weight to pull line from the reel. At this point it's also wise to let the student know that in this case, the fish will strike the fly but won't hold onto it. The fly looks like food, but it does not smell or taste or feel like food, so a good, quick hook set is critical.

Cast the fly and bobber out among the fish. Watch the fly carefully. Often a fish will take the fly just after it hits the water. If you are using a floating fly like a grasshopper imitation or Bluegill Bug, the fish will probably eyeball the fly for a few seconds and then either take it or lose interest. When using a sinking fly like the San Juan Worm or Hare's Ear Nymph, or with any of the saltwater flies, the fly will sink and the fish may take it as it sinks. In either case, if a fish takes the fly, have the student set the hook by either reeling very quickly or by raising the rod tip enough to tighten the line. They probably won't react quickly enough the

The final step in the education of a fly fisher is to catch a sunfish on a fly rod.

first time, which is fine because they'll see what happens with a fly when you don't set the hook quickly—no connection.

If you get no love right after the fly hits the water, move the fly by asking the student to make just a few cranks of the reel, enough to move the bobber an inch or so. Let the fly settle again. Repeat these gentle movements until the fly gets too close to you or you hook a fish. With most of the saltwater species, you'll need to keep up a pretty fast retrieve to tempt the fish. With freshwater fish like sunfish or bass, a start-stop motion is more likely to entice a strike, but if not, try a steady retrieve for them as well. The lessons your student should learn here are:

1. You need some kind of weight to get a fly out to the fish.

2. It pays to experiment with different kinds of retrieves.

3. When using an artificial fly, you have to strike immediately or the fish will spit it out.

Step 3: Break Out the Fly Rod

At this point, if you have never fished with a fly rod and are learning yourself, it's wise to visit chapter 3 briefly to learn how to attach a leader to a fly line, how to make a basic overhead cast or roll cast, and how to retrieve line by hooking it over the finger of your rod hand. That's all you need to know at this point. If you're a fly fisher and are teaching someone else, you're all set to go on to this step.

To make the transition from the push-button rod and bobber to the fly rod, show your student the thick fly line and explain how the fly line is the weight that casts the fly out to the fish. It's like a long, flexible bobber, which is why the casting motions used with a fly rod are different from those used for a push-button or spinning rod. In conventional fishing you're flicking a weight out into the water, but with a fly rod the weight you cast is long and flexible and has to form a loop in the air to get the fly out to the fish. Then show your student the leader, explaining that fish probably won't take a fly attached to the heavy fly line. It's too thick, and the fly would land too hard if just attached to the end of the line. But with a leader, you get a long, flexible, relatively invisible connection that keeps the fly looking like a bug or minnow that is not attached to a piece of rope. Explain that the rod, line, and leader are all tapered from their heaviest point closest to you to the thinnest point on the far end.

Before you tie the fly on the leader, show your student how much more efficient it is to cast a fly with a fly rod as opposed to the bobber arrangement. Show them how you can pick up a cast and move it to a different spot without reeling in any line, and how the water is disturbed much less by a line and leader hitting the surface than a big plastic bobber. Explain how the line hand is what gives the fly movement through the water, and demonstrate how you hook the line over your finger to keep complete control over the line.

Remove the fly from the bobber rig and tie it on the end of your leader with the same knot you used to tie it to the push-button outfit. Most likely this was a clinch knot, which your student will already know if they've fished with conventional tackle. I always notice a sense of relief when you show them you use the same knot for fly fishing, because it

Be prepared to help your student set the hook the first time they try fly fishing.

alleviates apprehension that they'll have to learn a bunch of new, complicated knots.

If you've never used a fly rod before, get about 15 feet of line out of the tip of the rod. Strip some line from the reel and shake out line by wiggling the rod tip, or put the rod down and physically pull line out beyond the tip. Flick the fly out to the fish with a simple overhead cast, roll cast, or any movement of the fly rod that gets it out in front of you. If you're working with a student, hand them the rod and cast by standing behind them and making a quick cast with both of you holding the rod. Yes, they've never cast a fly rod before and it seems counterintuitive to take someone fishing with a fly rod when they've never had a casting lesson, but I think the whole process of learning to cast and retrieve line makes so much more sense after someone has actually caught a fish with a fly rod, even with someone else playing backup the whole time. I've seen too many graduates of a fly-casting course get to the water and throw up their hands saying, "Now what?" They learned a bunch of basic drills in a vacuum that didn't make much sense on the water.

Trout, even those living in ponds and fed pellets, are often difficult to catch and should be avoided on those critical early fishing trips — even though everybody wants to catch them!

Get the fly out in front of the fish with about a 20-foot cast, and keep the rod tip low, explaining to your student that line control is an essential part of the game, and with the exception of stream fishing, the rod tip should always be just an inch or so above the water. You can even have them keep the tip of the rod underwater, especially if it's windy, to help maintain a tight line. Students invariably want to keep the rod tip high above the water, which makes it difficult to make a cast, keep control of the line, and hook fish. Get the line hooked over a finger on the rod hand and show them how to pull line through the water. They will probably miss their first half-dozen strikes, so be ready to tighten the line or raise the rod tip yourself. Once a fish is hooked, back off and let them enjoy the game. Let them feel the fish and learn how to control the fish by moving the rod tip. And be ready with a camera, because it's rare not to see a smile of amazement the first time someone plays a fish on a fly rod.

At this point in the game, anything goes as long as it's safe. Your student's first reaction when a fish is hooked will probably be to walk backward to get it to the bank, as the reflex to bring a fish to the shore by reeling or stripping line has not been logged into his or her muscle memory yet. That's fine—sunfish are hardy creatures and dragging one a few feet up on the bank won't hurt it a bit. And if your student has problems with casting but wants to use the fly rod as an expensive cane pole, just dipping the fly in the water, that's fine too. Your mission right now is to have the student catch a few fish on a fly rod, period. When they use the fly rod as a cane pole they'll soon want to get the fly out farther, which introduces the concept of fly casting as a concrete method to get the fly farther out beyond the tip of the rod, not as some abstract affectation that is supposedly "more sporting."

Let them put a worm or live grasshopper on the fly rod if they want. And while they won't be able to cast a worm or live grasshopper using a standard fly-fishing technique because the bait will quickly fall off the hook, it will teach them the lesson that artificial flies are a pragmatic choice when fishing with a fly rod.

You'll notice that for this first experience I made no mention of moving water or trout. I think moving water adds too much complexity to someone's first experience, and I have seen too many people worry about losing their footing on a slippery stream bottom or catching the fly in a tree during their first outing. You want to control a student's first experience on a fly rod as much as you can, eliminating any variables that will cause frustration or distraction. For the same reason, I'd advise you not to start someone off with trout at all. Even freshly stocked, pellet-fed trout can be notoriously hard to catch for beginners. When you observe pellet-fed trout carefully, you see them shy away from anything that does not look like a fish pellet sitting perfectly motionless on the water. It's really difficult for a student to maintain a tight enough line to set the hook even while keeping the fly motionless, and watching trout after trout nose up to the fly before turning away can end a beginner's first outing on a disappointing note.

Chapter 3

Gear and Casting:
Keep It Simple at First

When I talk to people who express an interest in fly fishing, one of the aspects that intimidates many of them is the vision from the cover of *Field & Stream* of an old guy wearing voluminous waders hitched up with complicated suspenders and attached to clunky boots, combined on top with a vest of a thousand pockets, festooned with all kinds of gadgets. In their vision he's usually smoking a pipe, peering at the water with the look a father gives his teenage daughter's boyfriend. But all that gear is usually extraneous and absolutely frivolous. Adult toys, nothing more.

If you are planning to teach someone fly fishing, or at least introduce her to the idea, don't scare your student off by loading her down with gear that she doesn't understand. It's true that many of us love the accumulation of gadgets and like to try different tools or brands of tippet material or formulas of fly floatant, but let your student work gradually into that world, if at all.

When my wife, Robin, decided she wanted to learn fly fishing after ten years of marriage to a foaming-at-the-mouth fly fisher, she found that she loved the casting and walking in the water and observing all the minuscule life on the water she'd been ignoring for years. But she admitted, "I really don't want to deal with all that gear. It's not something I'm interested in. Just get me a pair of waders that fit and pick me out a few flies that will work in the backyard." So I did. I didn't even let her have a pair of snips or some forceps to unhook the fish. I waited until she ran into trouble trying to cut a knot or get a hook out of a fish before I gave her the proper tools, and once she realized, after breaking off a few flies, that her leader was way too short and heavy, I slipped a spool of tippet material into her wader pocket. I waited until she learned by experience, on her own, how much of that gear she needed to carry.

Of course, my basement room is better stocked with gear than some fly shops because I've worked in the fly-fishing industry since I was fourteen years old. So you do need to purchase or borrow the bare minimum before you begin fishing, or before you begin to teach a member of your family.

The Basic Equipment

Fly Rod

Fly rods are classified by length and line size. The physical weight of a fly rod means very little, because it's more a reflection of the type of cosmetics (the guides that hold the line to the rod when casting, the reel seat that holds the reel to the rod, and the cork grip that serves as the handle of the rod) than the business part of the rod, which is called the "blank." Most blanks weigh an ounce or two, so it's the finished look of the rod that determines its physical weight.

The length of the rod you choose is determined partly by personal preference and partly by the type of fishing it is intended for. Rods shorter than 8 feet long are designed for fishing small, brushy streams and are specialist rods that are harder to cast and harder to use to manipulate line once it is on the water. Rods longer than 9 feet are used for fishing very wide rivers and making casts in excess of 70 feet. They are also heavier and more tiring. So most of the fly rods sold and used today are in the 8- to 9-foot range.

The line size is a little more complicated. The fly line is the weight that casts the fly, unlike in spin fishing where you cast the lure. In fly fishing you cast a long, unfolding loop, and the fly just goes along for the ride. Every fly rod is designed to cast a particular size line. The weight of the line flexes the rod so that it builds up the proper energy to push the line through the air. A line that is too heavy for a particular rod will make

Different types of fly rods for different conditions. The 4-weight outfit on the left is great for trout and sunfish and is thinner and lighter. The 8-weight rod on the right throws a larger fly line (and thus bigger flies) and has the strength and power to cast 70 feet and handle a striped bass, steelhead, bonefish, pike, or largemouth bass. Notice the bigger outfit also has a larger reel, which retrieves line faster and holds a bigger fly line, as well as 200 yards of backing.

the rod collapse without recovering quickly enough to deliver the right energy, and a line that is too light for a rod won't make it bend enough to throw the line unless the caster puts almost herculean effort into the casting motions.

Common line sizes are rated from a size 1 to a size 12, and as the number increases the line gets heavier. (Actually the number goes higher than 12, as specialty rods for fish like giant sharks, sailfish, and tuna have been developed in sizes 13 to 15, but these behemoths are seldom used or seen.) Why do we need all these sizes? Delivering a fly is always a balance between power and delicacy—power enough to throw a fly the proper distance, and delicacy enough to deliver the fly without frightening a fish. For instance, throwing a fly big enough to interest a northern pike requires a heavy fly line, like a size 9. When you get to a fly that reaches 6 inches long, it does have some weight, but even more importantly it has a tremendous amount of air resistance, and you need some mass to push that fly through the air. A soda straw can fire a piece of wadded-up paper across the room, but try pushing a balloon across the room with the same tool.

Why not use a heavy rod all the time? If a 9-weight will deliver a 6-inch fly, it would have no trouble at all casting a tiny dry fly. The problem here is that trout, usually the target of tiny dry flies, are spooky creatures, and the mass of a 9-weight line falling anywhere near one is enough to send it bolting for cover. In addition, a 9-weight rod is a pretty stiff instrument, and fighting a 10-inch trout on a 9-weight rod is not much fun. So you choose the tool for the kind of fishing you'll be doing.

Is there a universal, all-around rod? Not really, but a middle-of-the-road rod like a 6-weight is delicate enough for most trout fishing, can cast a fairly large bass fly, and has the power to land a 5-pound bass in heavy weed cover. It's still a compromise at the delicacy end for shallow, clear trout streams, and it will have trouble pushing a frog popper into a 10-knot wind, but it will do the job for a wide variety of different fishing conditions.

Here is a quick guide to the various line sizes and their most common uses.

Line Sizes	Fly Sizes	Maximum Practical Casting Distance	Typical Species
1 and 2	$\frac{1}{16}$ to $\frac{1}{2}$"	40 feet	Trout and panfish, delicate conditions, clear water, small flies, no weeds, no wind
3 and 4	$\frac{1}{16}$ to $1\frac{1}{2}$"	50 feet	Trout and panfish, relatively clear water, some weed growth, light winds
5 and 6	$\frac{1}{4}$ to 2"	65 feet	Trout, panfish, small bass, shad, small pike and pickerel, windy conditions, longer casts, big lakes
7 and 8	$\frac{1}{2}$ to 3"	80 feet	Freshwater bass, smaller salmon and steelhead, inshore saltwater fly fishing for species like striped bass, bonefish, redfish, and sea trout
9 and 10	1 to 7"	100 feet	Large freshwater bass on big lakes, pike, muskies, striped bass and bluefish in open water, small tarpon, permit, large steelhead and salmon
11 and 12	1 to 8"	100 feet	Large tarpon, sailfish, marlin, large sharks, tunas

When push comes to shove, the world could probably get along just fine with six instead of twelve different line sizes, but twelve is what we started with back in the 1960s when this rating system was developed. I believe this is true because some very fine anglers I know who fish for everything from tiny brook trout in mountain streams to sailfish have rods for every other line size—in other words, a 2-weight, 4-weight, 6-weight, 8-weight, 10-weight, and 12-weight.

Casting can be taught and learned with any type of fly rod, but some are easier for beginners than others. Rod designers and engineers have learned that the optimum specification for normal overhead fly casting is a rod that's 8½ feet long and takes a 5-weight line. This has to do with the physical characteristics of fly rod materials and fly line density and a host of other things I don't really understand, but when rod designers examine what a fly rod has to do to cast a fly line easily, that is the configuration they always come back to. A rod that is shorter than 8½ feet is not quite as efficient at moving fly line through the air and forming proper casting loops, and a rod that's longer than 8½ feet brings added air resistance and weight into the picture.

I've seen people buy 5-foot rods for their kids, thinking this outfit is cute, but a 5-foot rod is a very difficult tool to use, and what it loses in mechanical advantage needs to be compensated for by using the muscles of the arm and wrist more, resulting in sloppy casting and a tired caster. Modern graphite rods, even 10-footers, weigh only a few ounces. Don't handicap your son or daughter by falling prey to the short-rod myth. Start them with an adult-size rod, and perhaps sand down the cork grip to a slightly thinner diameter to fit their smaller hands.

So for that first rod, get one for a 5- or 6-weight line that is either 8½ or 9 feet long. If you plan on fishing mostly for trout and panfish, go for an 8½-foot 5-weight rod, and if you want a more versatile rod for bass and trout and even small steelhead and saltwater species, get a 9-foot 6-weight rod.

Fly Reels

Unless you plan on starting out with some serious saltwater fishing (and I recommend that you don't), almost any fly reel that has enough capacity to hold your fly line will work. You should be starting out with bass and panfish—species that don't make strong runs—so a serious mechanical drag (a braking system used to put tension on the spool) is not needed. Later you

This standard arbor reel is simple and lightweight. It has few moving parts, and for most freshwater fishing, it merely serves as a line storage device.

may want to purchase a reel that sounds nicer or looks nicer or has a strong drag to slow down that 100-pound tarpon you've always lusted over, but that's an obsession, not a fish you want to chase with your family.

People usually put some skinny braided line called "backing" on the reel underneath the fly line. Fly lines are usually 90 to 120 feet long, and fish can run 200 yards before you can stop them, so you need extra insurance. But you should not worry about that now. If your reel and line came with backing already wound on, fine; sometimes you need some backing on the reel to help fill the spool so the line is not wound around such a narrow arbor and doesn't have such abrupt curls when it comes off the reel. I don't even bring up the concept of backing when teaching someone basic fly fishing. It's just more jargon to confuse them.

Most reels come with removable spools so that if you have both floating and sinking lines, you can just switch spools without needing to buy a whole new reel. And they all have drag adjustments, usually a knob on the side of the reel that turns clockwise to tighten the drag and counterclockwise to loosen it. Just set your drag in the middle and leave it there forever. As long as you can easily pull line off the reel without the tension being so loose that the line overruns itself on the spool, you'll be in good shape.

Reels come in different arbor types. Standard or narrow arbor reels are smaller in diameter but need more turns of the handle to bring in line. Large arbor reels are larger in diameter but wind in line quicker, nice if you fish from a boat or from a brushy shoreline where you have to frequently reel in line to keep it out of the way.

Fly Lines

We've already discussed fly line size. But there are also different line tapers, because a line that is level, or the same diameter throughout its length, would not cast very well. Lines are made in many different tapers, and the choice of tapers in some specialty lines is so confounding that even expert anglers get confused. The most common type of line is a weight-forward taper, and that's just fine for any kind of fishing you do.

Some fly lines float, others sink at various rates. Keep it simple. Unless you fish in big lakes or offshore in the ocean, you'll do nearly

You need the weight of a fly line (the thick white stuff on the right) to cast a fly, but in between the fly and line is a thin, clear piece of nylon called a leader that makes the fly look more natural.

100 percent of your fishing with a floating line. It's the only kind of line you should use for practice, and it's the line you should use for your first fishing trips. Get the line size that balances the rod you've chosen, and buy it in a weight-forward, floating version. You'll see a cryptic code on the fly line box that look like this: WF5F. The first two letters are the taper (in this case weight-forward), the number is the line size (in this case 5), and the last letter is the sink rate (in this case a floater). So if you have a 5-weight rod, impress your family by walking in the fly shop asking for a "WF5F."

Fly lines are also sold in different colors. Get a bright one that appeals to you (yellow is the most common bright color). Against the sky, fly lines are opaque and look pretty similar to the fish, so get a color that you can see well in the air and on the water to help correct your casting mistakes.

Leaders

Few fish will take a fly attached directly to a heavy fly line, and you wouldn't be able to thread a fly line through the eye of your fly anyway. You need a leader in addition to your line. A leader is a thin, tapered piece of monofilament fishing line that slows down the unfurling loop of your cast with its air resistance and allows the fly to land on the surface with a minimum of commotion. Once it hits the water, the leader acts as a relatively invisible connection between the heavy fly line and the fish.

There are a number of different kinds of leaders: knotted, knotless tapered, furled, braided, and poly. The easiest to use and understand are the most common type, nylon knotless tapered leaders. If you fish for bass and panfish, get one that is 7½ feet long, and if you fish for trout, get one that is 9 feet long, as trout are more wary than bass and panfish and you should try to keep the heavy fly line as far away as possible. Leaders longer than 9 feet are made but they are harder to cast, so don't bother with them when you are starting out.

The other, often confusing, characteristic of a leader is its tippet size. While knotless leaders are all one piece, ready to fish when you pull them from the package, they actually consist of three parts: the butt, the mid-section, and the tippet. The butt is the heavy part of the leader, the end that is looped so it attaches quickly and easily to your fly line, and it transitions seamlessly into a midsection where the leader gets narrower very quickly, followed by a long (20- to 30-inch) tippet, which is the fine end of the leader, the end to which you attach your fly. But because a leader is tapered without knots, you never know exactly where the midsection ends and the tippet begins without using a micrometer. It's not a big problem, because leader design is not an exact science. The tippet size is determined by the size fly you are fishing—not the length of your rod or your line size or your mother's maiden name. Bigger flies require heavier tippets to overcome their air resistance; smaller flies need finer tippets for delicacy.

Tippets are measured in diameter or breaking strength. Typically trout leaders are measured in diameter, while saltwater and bass leaders are measured in breaking strength. Rather than worrying about small decimals when we talk of leaders, we assign X numbers to diameters to make it simpler, as in the following table:

Size	8X	7X	6X	5X	4X	3X	2X	1X	0X
Diameter in inches	.003	.004	.005	.006	.007	.008	.009	.010	.011
Approximate breaking strength (pounds)	1.75	2.5	3.5	4.75	6	8.5	11.5	13.5	15.5
Balances with fly sizes	22–28	18–22	16–22	12–16	10–14	6–12	4–8	2–6	2/0–4

In line with keeping it simple, for your practice or first fishing trips, get a 7½-foot 2X leader for small bass and panfish or a 9-foot 4X leader for trout fishing. Worry about the other sizes later.

Tippet Material

Every time you tie on a new fly or break one off, you will lose a part of your tippet. Sooner or later your leader will get too short and heavy—you know it when the tippet gets too thick to pass through the eye of the hook you're using. This is the time to add a new tippet to your leader.

If you started with a 7½-foot 2X leader, tie about 20 inches of 2X tippet material to the end of your leader with a surgeon's knot. If you began with a 9-foot 4X leader, add about 2 feet of 4X material. Tippet material comes on spools and is not tapered like the leader you began with, which works because the tippet doesn't need to be tapered—in fact, it casts better when the last few feet of your leader are the same diameter.

Eventually you'll want to fish a fly that's smaller or larger than the one you started with, so it's a good idea to have a few different sizes of tippet material in your pocket. It's more important to have the finer sizes, because if you want to go to a bigger fly, you can always just cut your leader back a few feet, as the closer to the fly line you go, the thicker the leader.

Flies

Don't sweat the fly thing. Fly fishers like to make fly selection complicated because it makes us feel like we are outsmarting the fish, but in the real world most fish (especially the ones you'll start out chasing) are opportunistic. As long as your fly looks alive and is big enough to catch their attention but not so big that it won't fit in their mouth—and it moves like something that's real—you'll be able to fool them. It always helps to choose a fly that is close to something they eat every day because they'll be less suspicious of your offering, and it's also just plain fun to try to match the food they're eating. But even on a hard-fished trout stream, with supposedly selective fish, you can walk up and down the stream bank asking each angler what they are catching fish on, and chances are that every one of them is using a different fly.

Get some of the flies I mention in chapter 2, ask a friend, check with a local fly shop, or do some research on the web. Some of these sources might try to sell you more fly patterns than you need. Pick three or four, or pin your source down to the three or four best, and get duplicates. You will lose flies—in trees, on the bottom, or in a big fish that breaks your tippet. If you find a fly that the fish like, you naturally develop confidence in that fly and you pay more attention to what you're doing. If you catch a couple of fish on a size 10 olive Woolly Bugger and you lose the only one

You don't need hundreds of fly patterns. With a few essential flies like these, you'll be set for most sunfish or other small freshwater fish, bass, steelhead, and many of the gamefish that swim close to shore in salt water. Clockwise from bottom: Clouser Minnow, Crazy Charlie, Woolly Bugger, Grasshopper, Bluegill Bug, Bluegill Spider, Hare's Ear Nymph, San Juan Worm.

you had, you may lose your confidence and will spend more time wishing you had another Woolly Bugger than figuring out how to convince the fish that a Hare's Ear Nymph is just as tasty.

Forceps

Forceps or a small pair of needle-nose pliers borrowed from your workbench are essential. When starting out, or when teaching someone, all hooks should have the barbs removed. This makes it easier to get the

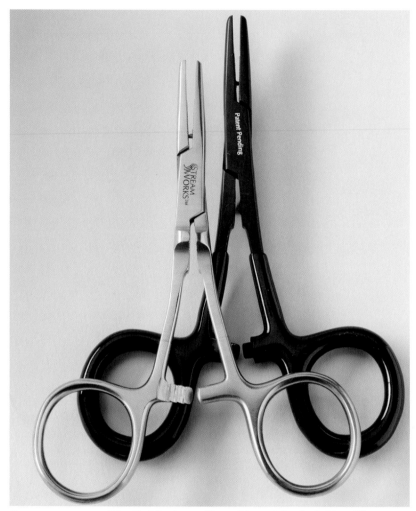

Forceps are one of the first tools you'll want to get for fly fishing. They make removing hooks from fish easier and are also handy when tying knots or crimping split shot. COURTESY OF ORVIS

hook out of a fish, but even more important, if you happen to bury a fly in your clothing or your skin, it will be much easier to remove. Flatten the barbs on all hooks by carefully pinching down on the barb until it disappears or you feel a slight click.

You don't have to get special snips for fly fishing, but these fly fisherman's snips are so much easier to use than scissors or nail clippers. COURTESY OF ORVIS

Snips

Cutting leader material with your teeth is not recommended. I did it for years and gradually wore all the enamel off my incisors. You can buy a special pair of fly fisherman's snips, or use the scissors from a pocket-knife. In a pinch, nail clippers also work, but the cutting arc on these makes it tougher to cut the tag end of a knot without also cutting another part of your leader, so use nail clippers with care.

Glasses

Sunglasses, prescription glasses, or safety glasses are a must when fly fish-ing, especially for novice anglers. A fly in the ear is a minor inconve-nience that at most could require a tetanus booster (I once fished all day

Everyone should wear sunglasses or some kind of safety glasses, whether they are casting or just observing from the sidelines. You never know what direction a fly will head, especially with high winds or inexperienced casters.

with a big saltwater streamer hanging from my ear and hardly noticed it). But a fly in the eye is a tragedy. On a cast the fly can be traveling hundreds of miles per hour, and one errant gust of wind, or just a bad cast, can drive a hook into your eye (or the eye of a spectator) in a microsecond. Fly fishers have lost the use of an eye from a single hasty cast, and at best it will require a trip to the emergency room, which will ruin your whole day. Flies, even barbed flies, can be easily removed from any part of your anatomy except the eye with a simple trick (see chapter 9).

The above list is really all you need to get started, in addition to the usual stuff you'd take on a picnic or a day at the beach, like a rain jacket, sunscreen, snacks, and something to drink. You will find a host of other gadgets and potions and special clothing, with fly shops and websites only too eager to sell them to you, but by keeping it simple at first, you can concentrate on learning how to fish with a fly, not how to drop some bucks in a fly shop.

Learning to Cast

If you're the rare individual who successfully taught your kids or significant other to drive a car, you might be able to teach them to cast a fly rod, but don't count on it. If you're even slightly impatient, don't even think about it. Great fly casters are not always great teachers. The Federation of Fly Fishers, or FFF (www.fedflyfishers.org), has a time-tested program of certifying casting instructors, and the test is *hard*. I'm a pretty decent caster and an experienced teacher, and I've never gone for my certification exam because I'm afraid I'll fail. These people take the *teaching* of fly casting seriously. Their methods are based on common sense and work for all individuals—they even have instructors for the hearing impaired. If you want to learn, or if you want a member of your family to learn, find one of their instructors in your town.

Another more expensive but more robust option is to send your family member to a fly-fishing school. These are classes that last anywhere from a full day to three days, and although casting instruction is stressed, they also teach the other basics of fly fishing, including knots, fly selection, reading the water, playing fish, and, of course, equipment selection. Classes are typically run by full-time casting teachers who benefit from a lifetime of shared experience; for instance, the Orvis Fly-Fishing Schools have been operating since the late 1960s, and their teaching methods have evolved constantly over the years. Many of these schools even employ video analysis so students can see their mistakes from another perspective and work to correct them.

Another option, just as good, is to find a clinic offered at a fly shop. Most of these are free or charge a nominal fee (mainly just to prevent no-shows), and the instructors are often either FFF-certified or are full-time, professional casting instructors.

Fly casting can be learned from books and videos, but these sources are, at best, an adjunct reference or a good way to review and fine-tune casting techniques. Nothing works as well as real-time feedback from a seasoned instructor who has seen thousands of people cast a fly rod for the first time and has developed methods and clever analogies to help a student understand how fly casting works.

If, despite my best efforts to convince you otherwise, you want to learn on your own or teach your family members yourself, what follows is a course in the two basic casts you'll need, the overhead (also known as the pick-up-and-lay-down) cast and the roll cast. This method of teaching is borrowed from Pete Kutzer and Truel Meyer, head instructors at the Orvis Fly-Fishing Schools as well as certified master casting instructors with the Federation of Fly Fishers.

The Overhead Cast
Set the Stage
Find a quiet place with lots of room, at least 100 feet long with clearance of at least 20 feet on either side. You will also need overhead clearance of at least 20 feet, so although fly casting can be practiced indoors, you'll need a room with a very high ceiling like a gymnasium or auditorium. Try to avoid spectators. Some people don't mind observers when they are learning new a skill, but most don't appreciate the "you won't catch any there" platitudes that bystanders can't seem to resist.

You don't need water to practice the overhead cast, but you will need it for the roll cast, so try to find a pond, fountain, or swimming pool. Cast on grass if water is not available, because casting on concrete or asphalt can ruin the coating on your fly line. You must also have a leader on the line. The leader is a necessary part of fly-casting dynamics, slowing down the unfurling loop at the end of the cast, and without a leader the fly line will whip around at the end, completely uncontrolled. Don't just attach a piece of monofilament to the line. Use a real tapered leader. The leader will get knots in it and will get abraded and ruined, so keep a special leader just for casting practice, and don't use it for fishing!

First Casts

Attach the reel to the rod and lay the rod down on the ground or have another person hold it while you thread the fly line up through the guides. The best way to do this is to double the fly line over instead of trying to poke the fine leader through the guides, and if the line slips back through the guides, its doubled thickness will prevent it from slipping back through all of them. Pull 15 feet of fly line out beyond the tip of the rod. This is important. A fly rod needs to bend to cast properly, and too often a novice starts with just the leader and a few feet of fly line outside the tip of the rod, and the rod doesn't bend enough to cast the line, making the initial casts frustrating.

Tie a ¾-inch piece of yarn to the end of the leader. Accuracy is paramount to fly casting, and without that indicator at the end of the line, it's difficult to see where the theoretical fly will land during practice. Accuracy, not distance, should be stressed throughout the lessons. Distance comes later, once the caster becomes more proficient with the timing of the cast.

At this point stress to the student (or remind yourself if you're the one who is learning) the three most important points when making a fly cast:

1. **The rod must bend in order to make a good cast.** The fly rod is a spring-loaded lever that transfers the energy of your casting motions to the fly line. In order to make this much easier and take

advantage of the tool you have in your hand, the fly rod must bend during casting.

2. **The rod tip must travel in a straight line when casting.** It doesn't really travel in a completely straight line during casting, but it should travel in as straight a line as possible when power is applied to the cast. If it doesn't, the rod stops bending ("unloads") in the middle of the cast and you waste all the power you've built up in the bent rod.

3. **The rod tip must be accelerated to a hard stop.** This is essential both on the backcast, when the line goes behind you, and on the forward cast, when you deliver the fly out in front of you. The hard stop is what makes the rod return from its bent configuration to a straight line, transferring all its energy to the fly line. If you can think "pop to a stop," you'll have the correct motion.

It is important to begin the overhead cast with the rod tip low to the water.

The rod tip moves to just past vertical and makes an abrupt stop.

The abrupt stop forms an open loop in the line.

Wait for the loop to straighten behind you.

Begin accelerating to an abrupt stop on the forward cast.

The abrupt stop makes the loop unfold in front of you.

After the loop unfurls, merely lower the rod to the initial starting point, low to the water.

Modern fly-casting instructors focus on what the rod is doing, specifically what the rod tip is doing, as opposed to worrying the student about what his wrist or forearm is doing. When you learned how to use a hammer, I doubt if your dad advised you what to do with your wrist or your forearm. He probably told you to keep your eye on the nail and to accelerate to a stop (or something of that nature), and not to initiate the hammer stroke with your forearm and then use the wrist at the last minute to add acceleration to the stroke—which, by the way, is the same motion you use to cast a fly rod and an appropriate analogy. And it's the rod tip that directs the fly line, not the handle of the rod. To push the hammer analogy just a little more, you don't worry about the handle of a hammer when learning to use it either. You concentrate on where the business end of the tool ends up (hopefully not on your finger).

It's probably a good idea to watch a fly cast in slow motion in a video, or at least watch a good fly caster in action, to understand what happens throughout the cast. A good caster begins the cast with the rod tip low to the water, and starts slowly. As soon as the line begins to move, the caster accelerates very quickly, lifting the line from the water. The rod at this point is bent deeply, with the tip facing forward. The caster then stops the rod tip abruptly just past his or her shoulder. At this point the rod tip returns to its state of rest, unbending quickly, transferring the energy to the fly line, which begins to form a loop with its open end facing forward. This loop begins at the rod tip and travels through the line to the leader. In a good cast the upper and lower sides of the loop are parallel and never touch. The rod tip does not move as the loop unrolls, but it is poised and ready to make the forward cast. At the instant the entire line has straightened behind the caster (it actually helps to think of this as happening just before the loop completely unrolls because it takes a fraction of a second for your arm to react), the forward cast begins.

A good backcast is straight and parallel to the ground at its completion. At this point the caster initiates the forward cast, beginning slowly and again accelerating to a firm stop when the rod tip hits eye level in front of the caster. As the caster makes the firm stop, the rod, which was bent from the weight of the backcast pulling on it, again straightens and the line forms another loop, which unrolls in a fraction of a second. The air resistance of the line and leader allow them to drop to the water with a minimum of disturbance, and the caster follows through by passively lowering the rod tip to the water without adding any power to it.

That's the way it is supposed to look. Your first attempts will vary. Most likely your biggest mistake will be bringing the rod tip back too far on the backcast, which directs the line onto the ground behind you and unloads all the energy built up in the line. It usually comes from bending the wrist too much on the backcast, but don't worry so much about your wrist—worry about where the rod tip is directing the line. Fly casting is a combination of wrist and forearm muscles, and some people use more wrist than others. You can cast with only your forearm and you can cast with only your wrist, but neither method is pretty or efficient.

It's perfectly OK to turn around and look at your backcast; in fact, you should. Make sure that the backcast stays parallel to the ground and that you begin the forward cast just before the line straightens behind you. It may help to drop one foot back so that it's easy for you to turn your body to check the backcast.

You may have heard casters mention "10 o'clock, 2 o'clock" when describing the casting motions. In other words, imagine a big clock off to your side, with 12 o'clock straight overhead, 3 o'clock directly behind you, and 9 o'clock straight out in front of you. Most instructors today no longer use that analogy because over the years they have found that it confuses novice casters, and it also suggests that the rod tip should describe an arc during the cast, which robs the cast of the energy it needs to develop in the bent rod. When power is applied to the cast, either on the backcast or the forward cast, the rod tip should describe a straight line in the air. One analogy that instructors use is that when applying power to the overhead cast, you should think of the rod tip as a paintbrush, and you want to paint a line with the tip of the rod on a straight ceiling rather than on the ceiling of an igloo. You can carry this analogy further by pretending to paint the ceiling and at the end of the stroke, splat a gob of paint behind you on the backcast and on the wall in front of you on the forward cast.

The other reason the "10 o'clock, 2 o'clock" ditty gets casters into trouble is that most novices begin their cast with the rod tip too high. If you begin a cast with the rod tip in the 10 o'clock position in front of you, you are forced to move all the line off the water and behind you in a very short arc, since you have to stop the rod tip just past the vertical to keep the line off the ground behind you. You just plain run out of room. Beginning the cast with the rod tip just above the water enables you to begin bending the rod earlier, giving you more room to make a smooth acceleration instead of a jerky heave back over your shoulder.

Just as the rod tip should move in a straight horizontal line during the cast, it should also move in a straight vertical line. In other words, don't let the rod tip drift back behind your body on the backcast or swing around in front of you on the forward cast. This straight line can be completely vertical or it can be canted off to the side as far as 90 degrees from the vertical, which is handy for casting under trees or to keep your line below the wind on a breezy day. Just make sure that the rod slices a straight path through the air and follows that straight path in both directions. Everyone develops his or her own unique style of casting, with most people using a slightly side-armed cast. You will develop your own style of casting in time, and no two casters look exactly the same.

Practice casting by making a cast, thinking about what you did, taking a break, then making another cast. Rest in between. Don't make cast after cast without thinking about it, and don't attempt to false cast until you are perfectly comfortable with the overhead cast.

False Casting

False casting is making a series of casts in the air without letting the line touch down in front and is used to change direction or to work out line on longer casts. You won't need this for your family outings until you venture into dry-fly trout fishing or fishing on big open water. False casting too early in the game only creates problems, as the longer you keep line moving through the air, the greater the chance everything will fall apart.

Everyone wants to false cast as soon as they pick up a rod, waving the line back and forth in the air like Brad Pitt (actually his stunt double) in

A River Runs Through It. False casting is an essential tool for working out more line and for changing the direction of a cast, but it should be used sparingly. Nearly every angler I see on the water false casts too much. A good rule of thumb is to never false cast more than three times in any given presentation.

To false cast, make a standard overhead cast without following through at the end. Make a good backcast, then a forward cast, and just before the line unrolls in front of you, begin another backcast, make that backcast as usual, then either make one final false cast or drop the rod and follow through to bring the line to the water. The casting motions should be in a short arc and more concise, and the line should never drop below your shoulders.

It's essential that you develop a good overhead cast, picking up and laying down the line, before you attempt false casting. The timing on a false cast is even more critical than a simple overhead cast, because any mistake you make during a false cast is difficult to correct while the line is moving through the air. Practice false casts with a short line, no more than 30 feet, and only make two or three false casts at a time.

Shooting Line to Increase Distance

I haven't touched on what you should do with your non-casting hand (usually called the "line hand") during the whole process. The best approach at first is to hold the line in your non-casting hand and keep it comfortably at your side. Avoid the temptation of following the rod up to the vertical with the line hand ("shaking the maracas," as casting instructor Pete Kutzer calls it) because you'll soon need to use your line hand for controlling the line right after you finish the cast.

Let's work on that now. Pull about 5 more feet of line from the reel. Hold this excess line so that it falls below your line hand—in other words, the line between the first guide on the rod and your line hand should be short and tight, with no slack in it—and all the slack line is between your casting hand and the reel. There should never be slack line between your line hand and the first guide, because as you begin casting, this slack must be taken up before the line puts any pressure on the rod, resulting

Shooting line is merely releasing loose coils of line held in your hand and feathering the line through the first guide. The trick is in the timing.

in the rod bending too late and not enough to cast the line properly, and the whole cast falling apart at your feet.

Now make a cast just like before, but as soon as you see the loop unrolling in front of you, loosen your grip on the line and let it feather through your fingers. The unrolling loop should pull the line from your hands and give you a few extra feet of distance. This is called "shooting line." It will take a few tries to get used to the timing of when to release the line. Most novices release the line too early, and all the energy pulls the line straight up in the air instead of on a forward trajectory. Wait until you see the rod tip out in front of you before releasing the line.

Try not to let go completely when you shoot line, because this often makes the line jump up and wrap around the rod. Feather it through your fingers or form an O with your thumb and forefinger to control the line and funnel it through the first guide. After you get the hang of this, make two false casts and let some line slip through your fingers after each false cast. You'll soon be working out line and gaining more distance smoothly and effectively.

The next step in maintaining control of the line is called the "anchor point." As soon as the line is done shooting through the guides, immediately move your line hand over to the rod hand and catch the line under your forefinger, or forefinger and middle finger. To retrieve line, or to make the fly swim through the water, pull the line from *behind* this anchor point while maintaining light tension on the line using your rod hand. Don't reach in front of your rod hand, which is a common reflex when first starting out. Always pull line from behind the rod hand—it gives you much better control.

Now when you make another cast, straighten the finger of your line hand and bring your line hand over, transferring control of the line to your line hand. You've probably done some spin fishing—think of the anchor point on your rod hand as the bail of a spinning reel. As soon as you complete a cast you close the bail (transfer the line to the finger of your rod hand), and just before you make another cast you open the bail (transfer the line back to your line hand).

The Five Most Common Casting Mistakes

Here are the most common mistakes novices make when learning to cast a fly rod, based on the observation of thousands of students over the years in the Orvis Fly-Fishing Schools. Watch for these in your own casting or when watching family members struggling with their technique.

1. **Rod tip back too far.** That rod tip should stop so that the backcast stays high and parallel to the ground. It's not necessarily at 2 o'clock, as you can make a perfectly good cast stopping the rod at anywhere from 1 o'clock to 3 o'clock. It's when the rod tip directs the line down behind the caster that he or she gets into trouble, whether it's from using too much wrist or just poking the rod too far back with the forearm.

2. **Starting the cast too high.** Make sure the rod tip begins below waist level on the backcast so that the acceleration to a stop is smooth rather than jerky.

3. **Power too early.** On both the backcast and forward cast, it's an *acceleration* to a firm stop, not a deceleration. Adding the maximum power too early in the stroke forms what is called a "tailing loop," where the fly catches on the line, leader, or rod. If someone catches their fly on the line, it's a sure sign they are applying the maximum power too early.

4. **Throwing the cast.** On the forward cast the arm should not be thrown way out in front of the caster, as you would in throwing a baseball. If you see someone completing a cast with their casting arm straight out in front of them, it's a sure sign they're throwing the cast. It's a natural tendency because we are trying to throw something out in front of us. It just doesn't work with a fly rod. At the completion of the cast, the casting arm should be bent at the elbow, not straight.

5. **Not coming to an abrupt stop and waiting for the backcast to straighten.** The backcast must straighten behind the caster before the forward cast is begun. Not waiting for the backcast to straighten makes a distinctive cracking sound, and if the entire backcast is not allowed to straighten, the rod does not have enough tension on it to bend properly and transfer its energy to the fly line. Letting the backcast straighten and pull on the fly rod makes the forward cast almost effortless.

The Roll Cast

Like the overhead cast, the roll cast is a two-part cast with a distinct pause in between, except the pause in the roll cast is a complete one, where the line stops moving. And the roll cast has no backcast (the line never goes more than a few feet behind the caster), so it is great when people or objects are behind a caster. The roll cast, unlike the overhead cast, can be made even if the line in front of the angler is a mess of slack. Some teachers argue that it should be taught first because it can be used to set up the line properly for a good overhead cast. However, in order to deliver the line properly with a roll cast, it's important to understand the principles of the speed-up-to-a-stop motion and the straight-line path of the rod tip. The principle behind these is easier to teach with an overhead cast. But if you find the roll cast easier to learn or teach before the overhead cast, give it a try.

At first the roll cast seems like a godsend to the novice caster, and I invariably hear "Oh, I'm going to just use that one all the time" from students. The roll cast has its advantages: no backcast to catch in the trees, no line whistling over your head, and no timing issues on the backcast to worry about. But the roll cast also has its limitations. It's not as accurate as the overhead cast and can't throw a fly as far, especially in the wind, and you have to make repeated roll casts when changing direction more than about 10 degrees in either direction. It is also difficult to gain extra distance with the roll cast because you can't shoot as much line with it. Besides, from a purely aesthetic perspective, it doesn't form those pretty loops or deliver the fly to the water with barely a whisper on the surface, so it's nowhere near as satisfying to perform or to watch.

Set the Stage

First, you need water. The roll cast relies on an anchor point, with water holding the line in place, so you must be standing on the edge of the water, within a foot or so of shore. The surface tension of the water holds this anchor point in place. If you try to practice a roll cast on grass or pavement, the line slides too easily, putting less of a bend in the rod and making the cast fall into a puddle in front of you.

First Casts

Begin the cast by slowly bringing the rod tip off to your side, away from your body a bit, raising your arm with the wrist in line with the forearm (not bent), until your wrist is opposite your ear. Pretend you are talking on the phone with someone but they're yelling at you—your wrist and arm will be in the perfect position. Slide the rod tip back slowly until you have a loop of line behind the rod, forming a semicircle. Some casters call this a "D-loop": The straight part of the D is the rod, and the arc is the line

Begin the roll cast by slowly bringing the rod back and slightly to the side.

Making a roll cast uses the same motion as the forward part of the overhead cast.

The line will then unroll in front of you.

behind the rod. The anchor point, where the line leaves the water, should be just in front of you and off slightly to one side.

Now wait until the line stops moving. You could wait for five or ten minutes if you wanted, as long as there is no wind to blow that D-loop out of position. Next, just as you did with the overhead cast, accelerate the rod tip to an abrupt stop straight out in front of you. Make that quick "pop to a stop"—it's exactly the same motion as the forward part of the cast in the overhead cast. Follow through with the cast after the power and the stop by bringing the rod tip down to just above the water. At this point you'll be set up for another roll cast or an overhead cast.

Casting Games

I would estimate that about 80 percent of the people who fly fish are barely adequate casters. Polished fly casting requires practice, and while little casting skill is needed for the family fishing suggestions given in this book, such as fishing for panfish or small bass or stocked trout, there are some aspects of fly fishing that require competent casting skills—casting over 40 feet, casting into a strong wind, placing the fly in a circle the size of a dinner plate from 50 feet away. If you plan on fishing in salt water, or for salmon and steelhead, or for trout in low, clear water, you will eventually realize that fishing a few times a year does not give you enough practice to place the fly where it should land.

If you plan on taking your fly-fishing trips to the next level, everyone in the family should practice. I doubt if anyone would play golf at Pebble Beach or St. Andrews without spending some serious time on the driving range and putting green, and fly casting is no different. Your casting does not have to be pretty, and everyone has his or her own distinct style, but if the fly does not go where you want it to, you just won't have as much fun.

I host a trip to Grand Bahama Island every year, and most of the people who attend are already competent fly fishers when it comes to fishing for bass in a small pond or casting streamers and nymphs from a drift boat, so they don't bother to practice before their trip. And most end up frustrated when presented with a fast-moving bonefish 40 feet away, when the fly must be picked up and cast accurately into the wind. Most of their problems arise from mistakes in basic casting technique, not in any kind of esoteric trick casts. They just have not polished the basic timing and arm motions needed for any kind of casting and have gotten away with sloppy casts for years because much of the fishing we do just doesn't require much precision from the caster.

Everyone can benefit from practicing their fly casting, and it doesn't have to be a grind. Even the best tournament casters practice almost every day, because they know that no cast is perfect and there is always room for improvement. So when you and your family are starting out on a long road to what will hopefully be a fulfilling, shared experience, some casting practice before a long-anticipated trip will repay you many times over.

Make it a game. Set a series of hula hoops, old plates, or napkins on the ground in your yard or at a local park. If you can find a place indoors with high ceilings and lots of overhead clearance, this can even be a winter activity. Put some of the targets next to obstacles like trees or walls,

You can play casting games anyplace you have enough room—no water required.

and place a length of rope on the ground pinpointing where the caster should stand. Tie a ½-inch piece of yarn to the end of a practice leader. Measure the distance to the targets if you wish, but since this is practice for realistic situations, just make the distance within the range of each caster's ability. Most fly fishing is about accuracy and not about throwing a fly line as far as you can. Then play the game like golf, where each caster goes through the course aiming for the lowest score possible.

Here are some suggestions for a few "holes" for your casting course:

Basic accuracy. Place two or three targets at different distances—one at about 15 feet, one at 30, and maybe one at 45. Each player gets ten tries to hit each target. Their score is the number of casts it takes to get the yarn into the hoop. This game is great practice for any kind of fishing trip and should be included in any practice course.

Obstacle course. Set up a course similar to the basic accuracy one with the easy 30-foot range, but this time place the course near trees so that the caster has to cast under overhanging branches, or make it so that a right-hander has an obstacle on his or her right-hand side and thus has to cast left-handed or has to dump a backcast on the target. Make the lefties cast in the other direction. This is great practice for a trout-fishing trip, especially one on small to medium-size streams where brushy banks present problems.

Timed casting. With an easy target, somewhere around 30 feet away, give each caster one minute to place as many casts as possible into the middle of the hoop. Or put three hoops down and give them twenty seconds in each of the hoops. Each caster begins with 30 points, and a cast that hits the target takes a point off their score. This game is valuable prior to any saltwater fly-fishing trip, where fish move quickly and in order to get a shot at one, making an accurate cast as quickly as possible should become second nature.

Chapter 4

The First Family Fishing Trip

The first family fishing trip should be a short one. It should be timed carefully to coincide with the very best time of the year for panfish, small bass, or juvenile saltwater species because your goal is for everyone to catch fish. If possible, I'd also advise you to take only one other person at a time on this first trip. Whether you are an experienced angler and your student is just beginning, or if both of you are beginners, too many bodies creates chaos, resulting in a disappointing experience for everyone. If you have two kids, or if you want to teach both your spouse and your children, plan a special trip with one of them at a time if possible.

I'll give you an example of how *not* to plan your first trip, and why. A few summers ago I was visiting the Colorado mountains with my father-in-law, two brothers-in-law, and their kids. Between us we had one adult who was an experienced fly fisher, one adult who had been on two fly-fishing trips, two adults who had never picked up a fly rod, and six children between the ages of five and nine who had done very little fishing of any kind, and no fly fishing. My brothers-in-law and father-in-law wanted to take all the kids fly fishing. And, of course, Uncle Tom was expected to produce. I was terrified.

I searched in vain for a pond full of sunfish or small bass. These species are the perfect target—they are not fussy about what fly they take, they're not spooked by the presence of humans, and they feed eagerly in the middle of the day. I searched high and low for a sunfish pond, calling my buddies at the local fly shop and poring over a map and the Colorado fish and game website. Unfortunately, at 7,000 feet the water is too cold to support bass and sunfish, as even at the height of summer, the water does not get warm enough for these hardy fish—they can survive in murky water, polluted rivers and lakes, golf course and urban park ponds, and drainage ditches, everything but at high altitude, where even shallow ponds are more suitable for trout.

My buddies at Fly Fishing Outfitters, the best fly shop in Avon, Colorado, took pity on me and invited us to some private trout ponds, stocked with trophy fish. Unlike the parents, who should have been smart enough, these guys also brought along candy bars and cold drinks and popsicles, which were lifesavers in the middle of the day. But trout, even stocked trout, are not the ideal fish for a first experience, and the whole event was pretty much a circus—and not the fun kind. Trout are more likely than

Throwing a bunch of kids and adults onto a trout pond for their first fishing trip is a guarantee for disaster.

sunfish or small bass to inspect their food carefully. They are also more likely to be selective about what they eat. Even stocked pond trout that are fed pellets to fatten them get selective to both pellets and whatever natural food is in the pond, looking with disdain on anything else, even if it moves seductively.

So even though the pond was full of stocked trout, the kids couldn't catch them. Heck, the adults even had trouble, though we could see scores of them cruising along the shoreline. We ended up putting nymphs on strike indicators, waiting until a fish swam by and inhaled the fly, but the fish ejected the nymph so quickly that the kids, with reflexes not accustomed to striking immediately, didn't have a chance to hook the fish by themselves. The adults ended up hooking the fish for the kids, but the trout were big and the kids reefed on the rods like you would to a shark that had just inhaled half a chicken, and, of course, almost every fish the kids tried to land broke off.

The result was pandemonium—whining, crying, foot stomping, and long faces. And the kids weren't happy either. If the pond had been full of sunfish, the kids could have cast to the fish with a couple of quick lessons. They could have watched the fish sidle up to a small popper or sponge rubber bug, inhale the fly, and hold onto it long enough for their undeveloped reflexes to hook the fish. And the fish would have been small enough for a five-year-old to drag up on the bank and admire before tossing them back into the water. Instead, both the kids and the adults had a miserable first exposure to fly fishing.

How to Plan That First Trip

Location and Timing

Location, location, location. Timing, timing, timing. Both are important. The most important part of that first trip is to catch a fish, regardless of whether your family member is a seven-year-old or a seventy-six-year-old. One of the ideas my fishing buddies and I mull over in those rare times on fishing trips when we aren't talking about fishing is the realization that fishing brings all of us back to our childhood. It lets us be that child who wants nothing more than to thrash around in the cattails looking for frogs, as much as we try to intellectualize the noble aspects of fishing—fly fishing in particular. And kids want to catch fish on that first outing, and they want to catch them *now*.

Sure, you can delight in the feel of water rushing around your feet and marvel at the way the fly line arcs gracefully through the air—finally—but scratch the surface and most humans are results-driven, and nothing instills more confidence and joy in fly fishing than a fish on the end of the line, that electric feel of a live creature you have fooled with an artificial creation, that you'll soon hold in your hands.

Plan that first trip to coincide with the time of year when your quarry is in shallow, clear water so the fish can be seen. For bass and panfish, this means when the water temperature first hits 60 degrees, which can be anytime from late February in the Deep South to late June in central Canada. At that period in their life cycle, sunfish (and largemouth and smallmouth bass, despite their name and size and prestige, are also members of the sunfish family) build nests in shallow water to lay their eggs. The female builds the nest first, and she is quite aggressive, attacking anything that could be a predator to her eggs or young. Once the eggs are laid, the male takes over. He not only guards the nest, but once the tiny black fry hatch from the eggs, he will guard them for at least a week as they stay in close proximity to the nest and their overprotective father, challenging and usually eating anything that looks alive and could be a nest predator.

When spawning, members of the sunfish family—including largemouth and smallmouth bass and panfish like bluegills, pumpkinseeds, redears, longears, and spotted and green sunfish—are almost impossible to frighten, so even humans looming over the nest and thrashing around in the water will not deter a bass or sunfish from striking. While filming a fly-fishing TV show, I had a fish biologist don a wetsuit and place an underwater video camera right next to the nest of a smallmouth bass. When the human approached the nest, the bass momentarily backed off until the camera was placed on the bottom. As soon as the diver retreated, the male bass returned to guarding his fry after a long stare

Nests made by sunfish show up like beacons, and the fish on the nests are very aggressive.

at the camera to make sure it was no threat to his offspring. Watching the footage afterward, you can see the streamer fly hitting the surface above the nest, at which point the male bass rushed over to challenge the intruder. The fly was immediately attacked, the bass disappeared as it leaped and fought the hook, and then just minutes later, after the fish was released, it returned to the exact same spot on the nest. I have no doubt that if we had stayed around for a half hour, we could have caught that same fish again.

You can find these nests easily if the water is relatively clear. When bass or sunfish clear a nest, all silt and sand is cleaned from a dinner-plate-size area on the bottom, leaving a bright, clear spot that shows up from quite a distance—even 6 feet deep if the water is clear enough. You may not see the fish right away. Sometimes you'll be too late and the fish will have already left the nest, but often the fish are so well camouflaged, as nature intended, that you have to stare at the nest with polarized sunglasses or from directly above to see them. Once the fish are spotted, drop

Biologist David Philipp stands ready with his fly rod while his wife, Julie Claussen, spots smallmouth bass on their nests with scuba gear. The bass were not frightened in the slightest.

the fly right on top of the nest. Sometimes a surface fly like a noisy popper will annoy the fish, which is the most fun, but often you have to let a sinking fly get down to the fish's level. They may inhale the fly as it drops to the bottom; if not, a few twitches of the fly will usually result in a strike.

Bass seem to be more aggressive than their smaller sunfish cousins. Where a bass will often pounce on a fly as soon as it hits the water or shortly after, sunfish may take some teasing. A small twitch followed by a long pause often works better for sunfish, and they usually take the fly as it is resting motionless. Don't twitch the fly again until the sunfish move away from it—as long as they are staring at the fly, there is a good chance one of them will take it.

Adult smallmouth and largemouth bass retreat to deeper water after the spawning season, although yearling bass of about 7 inches long will stay close to shallow water for much of the year. Sunfish almost always stay in shallow water all summer long, although they may be in deeper water when spawning. Look for them in shallow water that has protection from larger predators nearby. Lily pads and other aquatic weeds, downed trees, docks, and jetties all provide enough cover for sunfish, so while during the spawning season you might find them right out in the open in the middle of a swimming beach, at other times you can still find them close to shore. They may need more teasing than during spawning season, and you won't be able to spot those nests standing out like beacons, but sunfish and small bass are still your best bet for success.

Keep the Watercraft at Home for the First Few Trips

Unless you have no other choice to get close to fish, I'd leave the canoe or kayak at home, at least for the first few trips. Introducing another distraction is not a wise idea. It's less comfortable to move around in a boat, there is more of a chance that someone will be hooked with an errant fly, and the inefficient casting skills of a beginner can rock a boat beyond what is comfortable for the rest of the passengers. If you have no other choice, try to pick something very stable like a big rowboat or paddleboat instead of a canoe or kayak.

Popular Fish to Avoid on Those First Trips

I can't emphasize the importance of finding sunfish or small bass (or larger bass if they are around!) for the first fishing trip. Even if you live on the coast, try to find a freshwater pond inland. Saltwater species move every day, and the chances of finding them in any given spot are risky when compared to spawning bass and sunfish, which always stay put. Also, as I mentioned previously, even though most people who want to begin fly fishing are fascinated with the idea of catching trout and somehow feel that trout and a fly rod go together, save the trout for later.

Another common urban species, carp, live almost anywhere the water is warm enough, and although they used to be considered a trash fish, carp have become wildly popular with fly fishers. Not only are they a good size and can fight, but they are also wary and difficult to fool with a fly rod—which is precisely why you should save carp-fishing expeditions for later, when your family wants more of a challenge. In fact, carp are so spooky that a family trip is probably not a good idea even after your family has some experience, not unless you want to spread everyone out over hundreds of yards of water, because two people in one spot double the chances that carp will spook and leave the area.

Finding a Place to Fish

In most cities in North America, finding a pond that *doesn't* hold bass and panfish is more of a problem than finding one that contains them. Remember, you are not searching out a trophy lake popular with anglers—you want to find one that most serious anglers pass up because it only hosts small bass and sunfish. My friend Rich Merlino, who runs the fishing department in the Orvis store in Royal Oak, Michigan, advises his customers looking for a place to catch bass and panfish to look for ducks and geese. "Does the pond have ducks and geese on it?" he asks. "If it does, bass and sunfish will live there. Their eggs are sticky and they adhere to the legs of waterfowl, which transfer them from one pond to another in pretty short order." These species are incredibly hardy and grow quickly, and it doesn't take long to inoculate a pond. In fact, landowners often don't even suspect the pond on their property holds fish because "it was never stocked."

Ponds on golf courses, if you can get access to them, are sometimes gold mines. People hardly ever fish in golf course water traps, and because they never get stocked, no one thinks they contain fish. Fertilizer put on the adjacent greens fertilizes the water as well and makes it incredibly productive. Rich has found many golf course ponds that not only hold dense populations of naive bass and sunfish that have never seen a hook, but also sometimes hold bass of trophy proportions because they live their lives unmolested by anglers. Getting permission to fish on a golf course pond is not always easy, but if you're a member of the club or know someone, it is sometimes possible to gain permission to fish early or late in the day.

The greater Detroit area, according to Rich, has an incredible wealth of opportunities for the beginning (or advanced!) fly fisher. There is also good public access. Driving along Jefferson Avenue just north of the city,

Suburban ponds are wonderful places for both sunfish and bass.

fly fishers can find sunfish, rock bass, yellow perch, and largemouth and smallmouth bass at frequent pull-offs. Lake St. Clair offers the same mix of fish, along with big carp prowling the shallows and white perch boiling the surface while marauding small baitfish that leap out of the water as they are chased. There's crappie in Stony Creek Metro Park, and creek chubs, stocked trout, and even steelhead in the Clinton River. These are just a few of the opportunities, along with scores of lakes in the ring of metropolitan parks that surround the city.

But Detroit is just one example. How about New York City? Bass and panfish abound in the ponds of Central Park, especially the Harlem Meer and the Ramble. The same species are also found in Crocheron Park and Alley Pond in Queens, in Van Cortlandt Park on the border of the Bronx and Westchester, and countless other places. For the more advanced family trip, striped bass fishing in New York Harbor can be as productive as any place on the East Coast. In Washington, DC, right behind the Jefferson Memorial, is a bay on the Potomac with bass and bluegills. The Santa Fe Ponds and the gravel pit ponds near Chatfield in Denver have eager bass and sunfish just waiting to grab a fly. Green Lake, right in the middle of Seattle, has everything from bluegills to tiger muskies, and although the fly-fishing crowd in Seattle is typically preoccupied with steelhead and salmon, your family is much better off starting with panfish. Even Phoenix, in the middle of the desert, is laced with canals and ponds that offer fly fishing for bass, sunfish, and even respectable carp.

Name a city in North America and you'll be able to find some kind of fish to catch on a fly rod. If you don't know of a pond that contains bass and sunfish in your town, try the website of your state fish and wildlife agency (in some states known as the Department of Natural Resources, or DNR) or even real estate agencies. Many of these sites have "fish finders" where you plug in what you want to catch and where you want to go. Better yet, visit the website of the Recreational Boating and Fishing Foundation, www.takemefishing.org, where you can plug in a state or city and get an annotated map that shows fishing spots within the search range you specify. The map icons pop up a text box that shows you what species are present, making it easy to locate ponds with bass and sunfish.

Scouting the First Trip

Scouting by yourself before you take the family can make or break the first trip. Look for a pond or sluggish river with lots of room behind you for a backcast, which means not only free of trees, but also somewhere pedestrians are unlikely to walk. If your family needs to reach over a retaining wall or brush to land their fish, you can end up with broken tackle or tangles, so make sure the bottom of the river or lake has gently sloping shallows. Municipal parks with swimming beaches are ideal, and chances are you'll be fishing prior to the swimming season, so you won't have to worry about hooking bathers or passersby.

The ideal spot is a clear pond with plenty of shallow water that recedes gently into an area of mown grass or sandy beach. Even the smallest amount of brush on the ground can confound new fly fishers, and they'll get their fly line caught after they retrieve it. It's amazing how even a single patch of taller weeds can grab a loose fly line. You may have to drive around and scout several small lakes and then walk the entire shoreline before you find the perfect place. It's worth the effort.

Docks are also prime spots for that first fly-fishing trip. Sunfish and bass always hang around docks, and being directly above the fish makes them easier to spot. The novice fly fisher can even just "dap" the fly by extending just a few feet of line from the rod tip and dipping the fly into the water. This is an especially fun method for kids, but don't rule out its appeal for adults. After forty-five years of chasing all kinds of fish on a fly rod, I still get a kick out of dapping for sunfish off the end of a dock and can seldom resist the temptation! And don't discount the learning experience you gain by watching every move of the fish as they approach your fly.

If You Can't Find Bass or Sunfish

It's unlikely that you won't be able to find a pond with bass or sunfish in it relatively close to your home. In the off chance that you can't, or if you're looking for some different species to catch once you've cut your teeth on bass and sunfish, you have a number of options, depending on where you live.

Other Panfish

Rock bass and warmouth are members of the sunfish family that thrive in lakes, ponds, and rivers. They are as aggressive as any other sunfish and also prefer to stay in shallow water close to shore. Both species thrive in clear, rocky rivers as well as big lakes and small ponds. They are aggressive to almost anything that moves and eat small fish, crustaceans, and insects. Almost any fly designed for trout or bass will interest them as long as it will fit in their mouth. Rock bass also always seem to be on the

Rock bass are another member of the sunfish family that are always eager to take a fly.

feed and are less affected by changes in weather or water temperature than almost any other fish. These fish prefer a fast, steady retrieve, unlike the stop-and-go presentation that is so effective on the other sunfish.

Yellow perch are a handsome and tasty fish that often overpopulate a lake, causing them to become stunted and very hungry, which is a great situation for the beginning fly fisher. They are found across the northern United States and southern Canada, and because they feed on small baitfish, crustaceans, and insects—and feed most heavily in the middle of the day—they are prime targets for the fly rod. In spring and fall they frequent beaches with sand or gravel bottoms and always travel in schools. With careful stalking, a school can be sight-fished in clear, shallow water,

Small largemouth bass are more abundant and easier to catch than their trophy relatives.

which can be fun for fly fishers of any experience level. Unless you're a vegetarian, you can take home a batch of them for dinner, and when quick-fried in hot oil and eaten with cocktail sauce, they're reminiscent of shrimp. During the summer they retreat to depths of 20 to 30 feet and are thus not easily caught on a fly rod.

White bass are a larger schooling panfish that are more closely related to the saltwater striped bass than to largemouth and smallmouth bass. They feed mostly on small baitfish, but will rise to insects during a heavy hatch. They are most accessible to the fly fisher in large clear-water lakes and reservoirs in the central United States in the spring when water temperatures hit 50 degrees, when they migrate into the mouths of tributary streams on their spawning runs. White bass have also been crossbred with saltwater striped bass in hatcheries, and this crossbreed is called a "whiper." In summer they chase schools of small baitfish in open water, thus making them more difficult and less predictable. They can be caught after the spawning season by looking for schools feeding on the surface on schools of baitfish (look for birds diving) or by fishing deep with a sinking line and small streamers.

White perch, originally a brackish water panfish of the Atlantic coast, have been transplanted to strictly freshwater environments where they have become successfully landlocked, especially in lakes in New England and the Lake Ontario region. They are often the first fish to move aggressively to a fly in the spring, when they prowl the shallows looking for baitfish and crayfish. I have a special fondness for them, as this is the first fish I caught on worms with my dad, and in my early teens I learned fly fishing chasing these aggressive fish in the bays along the shore of Lake Ontario.

Large Minnows

Don't laugh. Carp are technically minnows and can reach upwards of 30 pounds, even in small lakes, but as I mentioned previously, carp are not for the novice. However, other members of the minnow family grow to a size large enough to put a decent bend in a fly rod and are much easier to catch. The two most likely victims are creek chubs and fallfish. Creek chubs can reach a foot in length, while fallfish get up to 18 inches and 2 pounds.

Look for creek chubs in slow pools in almost any piece of moving water in the United States from New England west to Montana and south to Texas and Georgia. Fallfish are found in similar habitats but only along the East Coast south to Virginia. You can find these big minnows rising like trout, and they can be a great training ground for the future fly fisher, but they can also be caught by stripping a small nymph through the edge between slow and fast water in a stream. Although these species coexist with trout in healthy streams, they are also found by themselves in suburban rivers that are too warm and sluggish for trout.

Trout Fishing in Lakes and Rivers

As I mentioned earlier, I'd really advise you to avoid trout fishing for your first family trips if possible. Nearly everyone who picks up a fly rod has trout on the brain, though, or perhaps you live in a place where trout are abundant. For these first trips, try to find some freshly stocked trout. Later your family may learn to appreciate the beauty and aesthetics of catching stream-bred fish, but I'll bet that at first they could care less and just want to catch trout. Stocked trout, especially freshly stocked trout, are not as wary or as picky about what they eat. After a steady diet of food pellets, they've discovered that the hatchery guy is not going to throw them real food every morning, so they have to busily begin sampling all kinds of foreign stuff to find out what's edible.

In a lake or pond, the best way to start out is with a nymph or Woolly Bugger. Look for swirls that indicate feeding fish. If you don't see any activity, pick a spot near where you think the fish were stocked (usually near a dock or boat ramp) and have your family cast out as far as they can. Let the fly sink a few seconds and then retrieve it with a fairly brisk motion. Experiment with faster or slower retrieves until they either catch a fish or get sick of it, and if they don't find any fish in ten minutes, try a different spot.

In rivers, retrieving a Woolly Bugger is probably the best approach for stocked trout. This fly attracts attention and wiggles like something alive, and few trout can resist it. The advantage to fishing a streamer with action like this is that your new students don't have to worry about reading the water or trying to use the currents to get a natural drift. A Woolly Bugger is effective irrespective of what angle it is fished in relation to the current, and because it is constantly stripped, trout often hook themselves.

Best Fish Species for a First Family Trip

There are few places in North America where you won't be able to find at least one of the species discussed above for your first family fishing trip. In the following table, I've listed the most popular small fish that are relatively easy to find and catch. Remember, your objective is to get a fish on the end of the line as quickly and as often as possible, and you should save the more glamorous species for later.

Fish	Relative Ease of Catching (5 is easiest)	Distribution
Longear sunfish	5	Upper Midwest east to Lake Ontario and south to the Gulf Coast
Pumpkinseed sunfish	5	Northern and central United States and southern Canada
Redbreast sunfish	5	East Coast south to Florida and west along Gulf coast to Texas
Rock bass	5	Eastern and central United States and southern Canada, south to Georgia and Oklahoma
Bluegill	4	Throughout the United States and extreme southern Canada
Juvenile largemouth bass	4	Throughout the United States and southern Canada
Juvenile smallmouth bass	4	Throughout the United States and southern Canada
Redear sunfish (shellcracker)	4	Central to southern United States from the East Coast west to Texas
Warmouth	4	Throughout the Southeast and as far north as Minnesota
Yellow perch	4	Across the northern United States and Canada, south to northern California and northern Georgia
Creek chub and fallfish	3	Throughout the United States west to Montana
Juvenile speckled trout	3	Atlantic and Gulf coasts from North Carolina south
Juvenile striped bass	3	Atlantic coast from Nova Scotia south to the Carolinas, with some spotty distribution farther south. Landlocked populations have also been introduced in large reservoirs throughout the United States.
White and black crappie	3	Throughout the United States except for the northern Rockies
White perch	3	East Coast from Maine south to Virginia
Mountain whitefish	3	West of the Mississippi at higher altitudes
Chain pickerel	2	Eastern Seaboard of the United States from New Brunswick to Texas
Speckled (sea) trout	2	Atlantic and Gulf coasts from North Carolina south
Stocked trout	2	Southern Canada and throughout the United States except for the Deep South
White bass	2	Eastern and central United States from Maine south to Texas

Habitat	Tactics
Quiet water of streams as well as small ponds	Small poppers, sponge rubber bugs, and nymphs. Flies should be no larger than a size 12, as this is a small sunfish that can't inhale larger flies. Fish them slowly with a distinct pause in between strips.
Shallow water throughout the year, especially near some type of protection after the spring spawning season	Small poppers, sponge rubber bugs, and nymphs, fished slowly with a distinct pause in between strips
Streams and lakes, prefers slow-moving current. Can tolerate brackish water and may be found in estuaries.	Small poppers, sponge rubber bugs, and nymphs, fished slowly with a distinct pause in between strips
Rocky or weedy shorelines in all sizes of lakes, sluggish backwaters in faster streams	Nymphs, streamers, poppers, and dry flies, fished with a fast, steady retrieve
Shallow water almost anywhere during the spring spawning season, moving closer to weed beds and other cover in summer	Small poppers, sponge rubber bugs, and nymphs, fished slowly with a distinct pause in between strips
Shallow, weedy shorelines in lakes and ponds of all sizes	Small streamers, poppers, nymphs, and dry flies, fished with a moderate retrieve
Rocky shorelines in larger, cooler lakes	Small streamers, poppers, nymphs, and dry flies, fished with a slow retrieve followed by a distinct pause
Large lakes and reservoirs, in clear water near vegetation. May also be found in smaller lakes and sluggish rivers.	Weighted nymphs, fished on a floating line with a long leader or sinking line
Near brush piles and submerged logs and weed beds in shallow water. Best fishing is in early morning.	Weighted nymphs, fished on a floating line with a long leader, or streamers size 10 and smaller
Over shallow sand or gravel bottoms in spring and fall, deeper water during summer	Small, brightly colored weighted streamers and small weighted nymphs
Slower pools and backwaters in streams and rivers	Dry flies, small streamers, and nymphs, fished dead drift with the current or twitched
Over submerged weed beds in channels and over oyster bars	Small poppers or imitations of shrimp and baitfish, fished with a fast retrieve
Estuaries, shorelines, and saltwater ponds from May through November in the Northeast, year-round in the mid-Atlantic	Poppers and streamers. Usually a fast retrieve works best, but also experiment with a slower retrieve.
Suspended above brush piles and other submerged cover in water less than 6 feet in spring and fall, then along the edges of deeper drop-offs in summer	Weighted streamers 2 inches long or less, fished on a floating line with a long leader or a sink-tip line. Flies with weed guards are best because crappies are found in heavy cover.
Brackish estuaries and freshwater lakes. Shallows early in the season, over open water during summer.	Small white streamers, fished with a fast retrieve. Nymphs are also effective.
Cold, clear trout streams, often in slower water than trout	Small nymphs, fished close to the bottom with a strike indicator. Where one is caught, more will be around.
Shallow ends of lakes with lily pads and other large aquatic plants	Brightly colored streamers, fished with a very fast retrieve
Oyster bars, shallow flats and marshes, and mouths of estuaries	Small poppers or imitations of shrimp and crabs, fished with a fast retrieve
State parks, suburban lakes, and urban and suburban rivers where they are planted	Streamers, nymphs, and especially egg flies, fished with a slow retrieve. Dry flies when fish are active on the surface.
In spring, around the mouths of rivers and tributary streams in large lakes and reservoirs. In summer, almost anywhere in large lakes.	Small white streamers, fished with a fast retrieve

Don't Sweat the Fly Selection

Few of the fish you pick for a first family trip are picky about what they eat, as long as the fly is relatively close in size and shape to the food in their diet. Here are ten flies found in most fly shops that will serve you well without agonizing over the thousands of fly patterns available today.

Woolly Bugger streamer

Clouser Minnow saltwater and freshwater streamer

Mickey Finn streamer

Glo Bug egg fly

Conehead Marabou Muddler streamer

Bead-head gold-ribbed Hare's Ear nymph

Bluegill Spider sinking sunfish fly

Bluegill Bug floating panfish fly

Zonker streamer

San Juan Worm nymph

ALL PHOTOS ON THIS PAGE COURTESY ORVIS

Fly Pattern	Type	Sizes	Colors	Species
Woolly Bugger	Streamer	8, 10, 12	Black, olive	Trout, smallmouth bass, largemouth bass, rock bass, warmouth, white bass, white perch, crappie, striped bass, sea trout
Clouser Minnow	Streamer	6, 8	Brown and white, chartreuse and white	Trout, smallmouth bass, largemouth bass, rock bass, white bass, white perch, crappie, striped bass, sea trout
Mickey Finn	Streamer	6, 8, 10	Red and yellow	Trout, smallmouth bass, largemouth bass, rock bass, warmouth, white bass, white perch, crappie, yellow perch, pickerel
Glo Bug	Egg fly	10	Pink, brown	Trout, sunfish
Conehead Marabou Muddler	Streamer	8, 10	White	Trout, smallmouth bass, largemouth bass, rock bass, warmouth, white bass, white perch, crappie, yellow perch, pickerel
Bead-head gold-ribbed Hare's Ear	Nymph	10, 12, 14	Tan	Trout, whitefish, sunfish, smallmouth bass, rock bass, yellow perch, white perch
Bluegill Spider	Nymph	10	Black, chartreuse	Sunfish species, rock bass, warmouth, largemouth bass, smallmouth bass, creek chub, fallfish
Bluegill Bug	Popper	12	Red and white, black, yellow	Sunfish species, rock bass, warmouth, largemouth bass, smallmouth bass, creek chub, fallfish
Zonker	Streamer	8	Pearl	Trout, smallmouth bass, largemouth bass, rock bass, warmouth, white bass, white perch, crappie, yellow perch, pickerel
San Juan Worm	Nymph	12	Red, tan	Trout, whitefish, sunfish

Knots You'll Need

You will need just two simple knots for your family fishing trips. Someone in the family should know how to tie them, but I don't think it's necessary for everyone to know them. Knots are not that exciting to most people, and I've seen the thought of learning a couple of simple knots throw adults into a panic. Your family will have plenty of time to learn them later, once they see how the knots are utilized, giving them motivation.

The lore of fishing is filled with hundreds of different knots, all of them performing a half-dozen simple tasks, and half of those simple tasks are only needed for saltwater fishing. Fly fishers like to invent new knots, and experienced anglers love debating the esoteric merits of a Duncan loop over a nonslip mono loop. Don't let your family get hung up on knots (no pun intended).

Tying On a Fly

The one knot you need to tie on a fly is a clinch knot. If you have learned another knot that works well for you, fine, but start your family on the clinch knot. Don't even worry about learning what is called the "improved clinch knot," because it is harder to tie and is no stronger than a properly tied regular clinch. I especially like the clinch knot for beginners because you don't even need snips to remove it from a fly—just grasp the barrels it forms in front of the eye with your fingernails and pull them away from the fly, and the knot comes apart easily.

1. Pass the end of the leader through the eye of the fly. It does not matter from which direction. Leave yourself 3 inches of tippet beyond the eye of the fly (the "tag end") when first starting out.

2. Wind the tag end around the standing part of the leader (the part that goes to the line and rod), away from the fly, six times. Five is usually OK, but I like to take an extra turn just in case I miscount. Any more than six turns make the knot harder to tie and are not necessary. Make sure the loop just in front of the eye is open a little because you have to pass the tag end back through it.

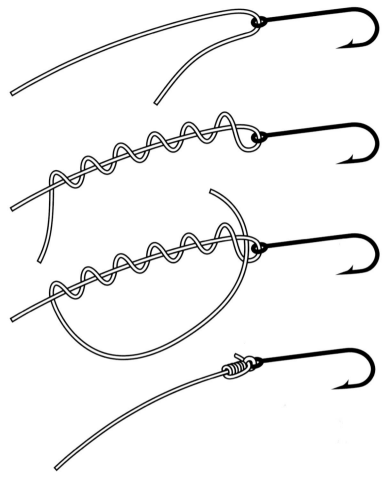

Clinch knot

3. Bring the tag end back toward the fly and through the loop you formed just in front of the eye. Hold it in place alongside the fly to make sure it does not slip back through, but don't pull on it.

4. Wet the knot with saliva to lubricate it and tighten with a quick, firm pull, pulling the standing part of the leader and the fly away from each other. Those six loops should jump together, forming a neat series of barrels. Trim the tag end very close to the fly. Always test your knots to make sure they are tight.

Tying Two Pieces of Leader Material Together

You'll begin fishing with a knotless tapered leader. Eventually, after tying on a bunch of flies or breaking off flies in fish or trees, the leader will get shorter and heavier. For bass and panfish this is of little concern until the leader becomes so thick you aren't able to pass the end of it through the eye of the fly. Later, when fishing for fish that are pickier, like trout or bonefish, a shorter, thicker leader can make the fish shy away from your fly, but for now let's stick to the more pragmatic problem of threading the fly.

So we have to tie on a new piece of leader material, which we now call the tippet. Your leader fresh from the package had a tippet already incorporated into its knotless taper, but now you have to add one, turning your knotless leader into a one-knot leader. (It's quicker and cheaper to tie on a new tippet than to replace the whole leader.) The easiest knot, and surprisingly also one of the strongest, is called the double overhand or surgeon's knot.

Pull 20 inches of tippet from a spool of tippet material that is about the same diameter as or one size larger than the end of your original leader (in other words, if you started with a 7½-foot 2X leader, tie on a new piece of 1X or 2X material), then tie the knot as follows:

1. Overlap 4 to 5 inches of your leader with the new tippet. Wet them with saliva to help them stay together and to lubricate them.

2. Keeping your new tippet and the end of the leader together as one piece, make an overhand knot, bringing both the new tippet and the tag end of the leader around and through the loop you formed.

3. Take a second turn in the same direction, going around and through the loop a second time.

4. Tighten the knot by holding both short ends and both long ends together in the thumb and forefinger of each hand, pulling the ends opposite each other until the knot tightens. Trim both tag ends as close to the knot as possible without cutting into the knot

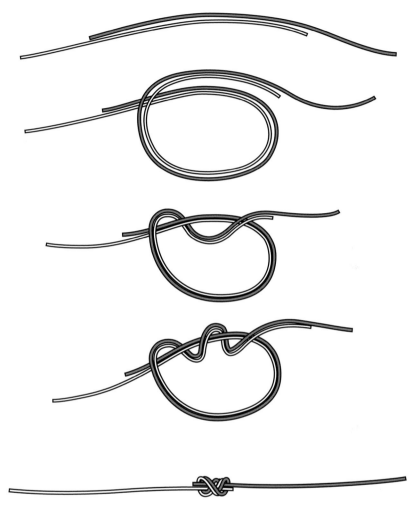

Surgeon's knot

itself, because tag ends that stick out from the knot may cause tangles as you cast.

Some people tie this knot as a triple overhand, which can be a bit
stronger when tied in very fine tippet material or when the two strands
differ greatly in diameter. For bass and panfish, two turns is plenty.

Line Control Is Critical

One of the hardest parts for beginning fly fishers is line control, but it's essential for hooking fish and maintaining control of the fly, especially if the wind starts blowing. It all begins with a rod tip low to the water, which is also the position needed to initiate another cast, so watch your family like a hawk. The only time the rod tip should be more than a couple inches above the surface of the water is during casting or when playing a fish.

By low to the water I don't mean waist level, I mean almost touching the water. In fact, it's a good idea to tell novice fly fishers to actually put the rod tip *in* the water, which makes line control so much easier. With the rod tip low and all slack line removed from the line lying on the water, every time they pull some line in by stripping it, the line and the fly move together in a one-to-one relationship. You pull 6 inches at a time, the fly moves in 6-inch darts. Pull shorter or longer, and the fly moves in shorter or longer bursts. This is important because you often need to experiment with different retrieve speeds, as you never know what kind of fly speed will tickle a fish's fancy.

Stripping line is accomplished by pulling the line through one or two fingers of the rod hand. By keeping light tension on the line and pulling from behind the rod hand, you are ready to instantly tighten the line when a fish strikes, either by pulling sharply on the line (like another fast strip, called a "strip strike") or by pinching the line and raising the rod tip until the line tightens and you feel the fish.

When stripping line you can either just let the slack line fall to the ground at your feet or hold it in loose coils. Coiling the line affords a bit more control and makes the line easier to shoot on the next cast, but at this stage in the game it's just one more thing to worry about, so I recommend you simply teach your students to drop the line on the ground at their feet.

Once a fish is hooked, bass and panfish can be played one of two ways: either by just stripping line or by first pinching the line against the rod, reeling in all the slack below the reel, and then reeling in the fish.

Keeping the rod tip low to the water and the line in your hand under control are essential elements in fly fishing.

When the fish pulls hard in the opposite direction, keep moderate pressure on the fish with the rod. If the fish decides to run hard, let it take line from your hand or the reel; otherwise, just keep pressure on the fish and bring in line when it seems to tire. Most sunfish can be brought in quickly, but a larger bass that runs and dives for cover may require a little give and take on your part.

Fast-running fish like big trout, steelhead, salmon, and most saltwater fish should be played from the reel because the fish may run with quite a bit of line, and you want the control and mechanical braking system afforded by a fly reel (called the "drag"). But that's not something you'll need to worry about on your initial family trips.

Releasing Fish

My personal bias is for all new anglers to keep and eat a few of the fish they catch. However, I understand that you and your family may have different ideas about killing and eating a wild creature, and I don't believe it's my place to preach to you on the pros and cons of catch-and-release versus catch-and-keep fishing. Even if you choose to keep fish for the table, you'll want to release smaller fish, or if you get lucky enough, you'll have so many fish for dinner that you'll need to release the rest. Quickly, safely, and efficiently releasing a fish is an essential skill for all new fly fishers.

Your first step should be to remove the barb on all hooks. This is best done with a pair of forceps or very fine needle-nose pliers, which you should always have with you on a fishing trip. Just place the tips of the pliers over the barb and squeeze until the barb is flattened. Hooks with the barb flattened hook fish as well or better than a hook with a barb because there is less resistance to penetration, but fish can throw the hook easier, especially on flies with weighted eyes like Clouser Minnows, but that's a good lesson for new fly fishers on keeping a tight line to a fish.

Fish should be played quickly, not to exhaustion. This is not a problem with kids, since they always want to get the fish to shore as soon as possible. Don't play a fish until it can barely pull and begins to go belly up; otherwise the exercise of releasing the fish may be futile, as the fish

When releasing a fish, cradle it in clean water and let it move off under its own power when it is ready.

may be exhausted and unable to maintain its equilibrium in the water. If you are close to shore and you have a nice sloping background, try to keep the fish in the water. Step right up to the shore, bring the fish to hand, and if at all possible, keep it in the water. This isn't always possible with kids because they like to hold their fish, and with most of the fish we've discussed, you won't hurt them by keeping them out of the water for thirty seconds or so.

If you're on a dock, in a boat, or along a steep shoreline, a net is a very handy device. You can often net the fish and keep it in the water while removing the hook. The best way to do this is to raise the net so that the fish is barely covered with water, and you can often grasp the hook and pull it out without having to touch the fish. This is healthier for the fish and is always handy around squeamish anglers who aren't quite ready to hold a squirming fish. Of course, a lot of the small bass and sunfish can be merely hoisted from the water, held in the hand, and then tossed back into the water. Most of the fish discussed in this chapter are really hardy and can be handled with moderate abuse without suffering major damage—especially the members of the sunfish family.

When grasping the fish, remember that sunfish, bass, and perch are called spiny-rayed fish for a reason—the spines along their dorsal fin are sharp, and the best way to grasp them is to gently cup the fish in your hand, making sure that all the spines along the back are flat along the body. If you move your hand from the head forward, it's much easier to make the spines lie flat. Largemouth bass, smallmouth bass, and striped bass have large jaws, and the easiest way to land them is to firmly place your thumb on their lower jaw. This makes a good handle and temporarily immobilizes them.

Pickerel, bluefish, and sea trout all have sharp teeth—never put your finger in the mouth of one of these guys, no matter how small it is! Soft-rayed fish like trout, fallfish, and creek chubs are best grasped gently around the middle of their bodies. Never squeeze a fish you intend to release, and always keep your fingers away from the gills of fish you plan to release because the gills are the most sensitive exposed part of a fish.

Once you have the fish calmed down and in your grasp, just back the hook out of its mouth. This is often possible with your fingers, but when a fly is deep in a fish's throat or firmly embedded in the jaw, you may need to use the forceps. Grasp the fly close to the bend of the hook and pull back—a barbless hook should come right out. If a fish is deeply hooked, way down in the throat or in the gills, you have two options: One is to cut the leader and lose the fly, as a barbless fly will work itself out in short order and the fish should be fine. The other option is to kill the fish for dinner and then rip the hook out with the forceps.

Once you are ready to release the fish, lower it into clear water away from any mud or silt you might have stirred up. Hold the fish in the water and gradually loosen your grip when you feel the fish begin to struggle. When the fish is ready, it will simply swim away. If it does swim a few feet but then turns belly up, grab or net the fish again and hold it in the water a second time until it swims away under its own power.

Chapter 5

Kids and Fly Fishing

Passionate fly fishers dream of having their kids turn into their best fishing buddies. It often doesn't happen at all, and when it does, the expectation seldom fulfills the dream—at least at first. Fathers dream of sons or daughters who spend hours on a Montana trout stream with them, quietly and patiently matching hatching mayflies with perfectly tied imitations they made themselves in the winter months. Mothers imagine the whole family on vacation in the mountains of North Carolina, bewitching wild trout with flies that own colorful names like Royal Wulff and Pale Evening Dun.

Dreams don't always come true. Sometimes it's just mom and son, like my friends Jane and Ronan Cooke. Jane came into fly fishing from an unusual direction. As a young landscape architect, her mentor was Alice Ireys, who created many major public garden spaces, including designs for the Brooklyn Botanic Garden and the New York Botanical Garden in the Bronx, but later in life was unable to walk. Jane was her legs. One day Ireys had Jane inventory some plants along a river, requiring that she wear a pair of chest waders. She fell in love with the sound and feel of the water and decided on the spot to learn to fish, and it seemed like learning to fish on a stream meant learning to fly fish for trout.

Jane's first husband had no interest in learning to fly fish, but after a divorce Jane attended the Orvis Fly-Fishing School in Manchester, Vermont, and then took to the sport with a passion, developing a circle of friends in New York and dating a noted fly-fishing author. When she remarried, her second husband, Patrick, already had plenty of hobbies that kept him busy, like cars, motorcycles, lacrosse, and reading, and had

If kids want to catch frogs in the middle of a fly-fishing trip, let them!

little interest in fly fishing, but he encouraged Jane to take her young son, Ronan, on fishing trips. First Ronan just dapped a White Wulff around the dock at their lakeside cottage, still in diapers. "Doing that actually requires less motor skills than using a spinning rod," Jane told me, "so it seemed like the right way to start."

Even though Ronan began fly fishing at an early age, it was not a straight-line path, and he still picks up a spinning rod if fly fishing gets too difficult or the wind froths the water. And Jane learned some tough lessons along the way. Figuring that since Ronan picked up fly fishing at such an early age, when he was five years old she decided to risk a salt-water fly-fishing trip to the Florida Keys with him and her friend, guide Paul Dixon. But all Ronan wanted to do was play with the live shrimp Paul had brought along for chum. The savvy guide taught Jane a valuable lesson, telling her, "It's OK—all kids gotta start fishing with their head in the bait bucket."

Patrick now accompanies them on fishing trips close to home, but Ronan is now twelve, and he and his mom search for more exotic challenges like tarpon in the Florida Keys and trout and salmon in Alaska. "We'd take him [Patrick] along more often because he likes to be with us on the water and read, but some of our trips are more remote and expensive, so we have to leave him home," said Jane.

It's worth the effort to involve your kids in fly fishing. Justin Coleman, a fly fisher and predoctoral intern in Counseling and Psychological Services at the University of California, Merced, looks at fly-fishing relationships both as an angler and as part of his professional development. Fly fishing is a great way to examine the interactions between couples, and between parents and children. When I asked him to give me a professional overview of the idea of a family fly fishing together, this was his assessment:

Fly fishing with your children, spouse, or whole family not only provides an opportunity to have fun and bond over a pleasurable activity but can also have benefits for your children's development. Research indicates that parent role modeling of healthy physical activity and outdoor participation has a significant relationship to the amount of time that children spend playing outside and exercising (e.g., Beets, et al., 2007; Bois, et al., 2005). Through positive modeling and instruction in fly fishing, parents can encourage their children to exercise and develop a lifelong interest in the sport.

Kids under Ten—Short, Sweet, and Simple

It doesn't start with fly fishing—it should start with just plain fishing. In fact, as Ronan proved to his mom on their Florida trip, it may not always be about fishing at all. Nearly all kids are fascinated by nature and the animals they encounter, and fish are only one kind of creature they can catch. If the fish are too difficult, they'll settle for frogs or turtles, and you ignore that fascination at your peril.

My father infected me with the fishing virus, not with a fly rod but with a worm and bobber, and for bullhead catfish and white perch in the bays along the southern shore of Lake Ontario. But my real quarry was frogs. Fish took too much patience for a four-year-old, but the frogs were always handy, just waiting to be pounced upon. I remember my father complaining to my mother that "all he wants to do is chase frogs." Dad was not patient enough for the circuitous path I took to becoming a serious angler, and by the time I was ten, he had moved on to golf, even while I was spending all my paper route money on rods and lures, getting up at dawn to ride my bicycle to find new fishing spots that were miles beyond the boundaries my parents had set for me.

My own son, now seven, fishes with me, but most of our fishing trips turn into turtle expeditions and frog safaris. I can only hope that eventually he'll develop the patience to fish for longer than six minutes, and I assume that he will develop the motor skills to cast a fly rod. Some kids can learn to cast a fly rod as young as three or four, but few have the patience to really fly fish in a serious way until they are over ten years old. When I tell people in the presentations I do for fishing clubs that I believe a kid should be about ten before any expectation of serious fly fishing,

Jon Luke's boys, Ben and Caleb, enjoy fly fishing with their dad because he started them out with lure fishing, and for their first fly-fishing trips he had them troll their flies behind a canoe, thus eliminating the complexities of casting. COURTESY JON LUKE

invariably someone corrects me and calls out that their son or daughter has been fly fishing since they were in diapers. It may be true, and prodigies do exist, but I wonder how many seven-year-olds are really serious about fly fishing for longer than a half hour.

Developing a child as a fly-fishing buddy takes years to ferment. It's about nature first, then just fishing by any means, and finally fly fishing. In chapter 3 I argued that, contrary to the way fly fishing is usually taught, with casting lessons on dry land for hours on end before getting fish on the line, the first step should be getting a fish on—otherwise the whole exercise makes no sense. And nowhere is this more important than with kids.

It *is* possible to start kids out right away with a fly rod. Find that spot where sunfish congregate near a dock, give your child a fly rod with a dry fly or tiny popper tied to a short leader, and let them dap for sunfish, where they can see the fish come to the fly, inspect it, and then finally inhale it. Dapping is done by just lowering the fly to the water directly under the rod tip, with no line or leader on the water. Only the fly touches the water. Dip the fly into the water, lift it out of the water, dip it in again, and then let it sit. This drives sunfish nuts, and they hardly ever resist it.

Start with Bait

If you can't find a suitable spot where kids can dap for sunfish with flies, grab a push-button rod, a hook, and a bobber. Go out and catch worms or grasshoppers. Don't buy your bait at a bait shop, as catching bait is half the fun for most kids, and sometimes more fun than the fishing itself.

Worms are found by digging in rich soil, turning over logs and rocks in damp areas, or by going out after dark to catch night crawlers—if you've never done this, your education as an angler is not complete. Water your lawn until it's soaked, or find a golf course where they water regularly, and then go out after dark with a flashlight with a piece of transparent red film over the lens. The flashlight should not be overly bright because too bright a light scares the night crawlers back into their holes. Grab the crawlers as close to the ground as possible, and don't pull immediately or you'll break the worm in half. It will pull hard against you, then will relax

When fishing with kids, never forget to bring a push-button rod in addition to the fly rod. The objective is for the kids to have fun fishing by any means.

its muscles—that's the time to pull in order to get the entire night crawler out of the ground.

Grasshoppers seem to prefer the edges of fields and along paths or roadsides, and if you go after them in the morning, before the sun warms their bodies, they move slowly and are much easier to catch. Once the sun warms the grasses, you will be better off using a butterfly net to catch them. You will need a butterfly net on all your fishing trips anyway, as you should ensure that you have something handy so kids can go off and catch critters as soon as they get bored.

Take a fly rod along on these bait-fishing trips, and just treat it as another way of catching fish. Make sure you take a box of flies with bright colors and patterns that really look like mice or frogs or minnows. Show your child the flies, tie one on, and make a few casts. If they're at all interested in fishing, they'll soon ask if they can use the fly rod too.

A word of caution on rods for children: Don't be tempted into buying a really short, novelty "kids' fly rod," and don't make a tiny fly rod out of just the tip section of a longer rod. These short rods are much tougher to cast and will only frustrate your child. A rod between 7½ and 8½ feet long for anything from a 3-weight to a 5-weight line will be perfectly fine for even the smallest child, and it will be easier to cast. Even the biggest rod in this size range will weigh less than 3 ounces, and although the reel weighs a little more than the rod, once the reel is attached to the rod, the balance point when the rod is in hand reduces the overall weight a child has to handle to less than a good-size frog.

Holding Their Attention

Gauge both the time of fishing trips and time with the fly rod in hand to the age of the child. When kids are under eight years old, thirty minutes of total fishing may be the maximum attention span, with perhaps

When fishing with kids, never forget the drinks and snacks.

an additional five minutes of fly fishing thrown in. If your kid shows an inclination to spend more time fishing (even some very young children have the patience to sit on a dock for hours), then by all means keep going. But never push it, never keep a kid fishing longer than they show interest. It's not about you at this point.

Parents should avoid fishing or fish sparingly on these trips. Resist the temptation to "show her how to do it." Demonstrate once and turn the rod over to your child, whether it's a fly rod or a conventional rod. They learn better by discovering in their own way, on their own time. And when they start peering into the cattails by the end of the dock, looking for frogs, it's your cue to take out that butterfly net and suggest a frog or turtle hunt.

Fly-fishing guide Colin Archer, in a letter to me, expressed the regrets of a father who taught his kids the wrong way. He wrote with the hope that he might guide the way for parents of future fly fishers. It was a poignant exclamation point to the idea that, especially for kids, fly fishing is just another way of fishing.

I realized I screwed up. I am a fly fisherman. I am a fly fishing guide. I love fly fishing. I believe in catch and release. I'm a little bit of a snob when it comes to bait fishermen and using things other than flies on "sacred waters" where I fish and guide. I have felt this way for about 10 years.

I started trout fishing about 25 years ago in New Jersey. I started with worms. I moved into spinners. I graduated to mealworms. Then PowerBait came out. I used to leave the streams and rivers with full creels almost every time out. I had more thin aluminum foil coffins in the freezer with hatchery trout fillets then I could eat. I was a harvester. I had a blast. Then I started fly fishing around 1990. Soon after, the movie A River Runs Through It *came out and I was gut-hooked.*

I married and had kids, two boys, and two years apart. If I could have I would have named them Norman and Paul after, you know, the two sons in 'The Movie.' As they got older and out of diapers I introduced them to fishing and of course they loved it. Then I moved them quickly into fly fishing. I got them neoprene waders. I had Fran Betters custom make them rods at his shop on the West Branch of the Ausable. They had the vests and hats to boot. I taught them bugs. I taught them hatches. I taught them trout. And here and there they would catch a stocked trout or two. I could never take them to the 'big' rivers like the Upper Delaware because they weren't ready for that, even though I always see kids throwing big Blue Fox spinners into the West Branch and catching big browns!

It took me a few years before I realized they didn't want to go fly fishing. In fact they didn't want to go fishing at all. When we would go away for a week in the Poconos I would take out my fly rod and catch 300,000 sunfish and bass. They didn't care. They made me get worms and hooks and bobbers. My thick head didn't get it, until I got it. I robbed my kids of all that fishing was and is supposed to mean.

I fish all the time, for work and pleasure. I live blocks from the beach. When and if I have one of my boys in tow when I go out with the fly rod, they look at guys throwing poppers and plugs and metal during a blitz while we're getting skunked on our fly rods and they ask me, "Dad, don't you like to catch fish?"

I have done more harm introducing my fishing "ways" to my boys than I know. I hope they don't make the same mistake with their kids. If I now want to spend quality time with my sons I have to sit down with an Xbox controller in my hand and play Call of Duty.

The reason I wrote this today is today is my son's 15th birthday, and I fished alone.

Hopefully you'll be in a better position to get your kids excited about fly fishing. My friends who have sons and daughters as their fishing buddies are some of the happiest, most fulfilled people I know. It's hard to overemphasize the importance of a shared passion between parents and children. When I pressed Colin to summarize what he would have done differently, here's what he told me:

> If I could do it over again, I would have kept them with their push-button rods longer and then moved them into spinning rods. I would have started them on worms and lures, and then introduced poppers and slowly worked in flies. I would have mixed in some stream and river fishing with more pond and lake fishing. I might have even taken them to the Upper Delaware for a chance for a big brown on a spinner! I would have focused on the time spent between a dad and his kids, not on entomology or casting lessons. Fishing should have been an experience, not a task.

Jon Luke, an art director and photographer who lives in North Bend, Washington, is a parent who started his kids out properly. He began by taking his sons, Ben and Caleb, fishing with topwater plugs on a Minnesota lake when they were six and seven years old, and luckily the lake was one where the fish responded well to floating lures. He feels that lure fishing, where it is productive, is more beneficial for getting kids into fishing because there is more action and less waiting for fish to bite. When he started them out fly fishing, he had them troll flies behind a canoe, just hanging their flies in the water so that he wouldn't have to worry about the complexities of casting. The kids got hooked on fishing with flies, and although they are both accomplished with a bait-casting rod and lures, they now prefer fly fishing.

"I think they pick up the fly rod first because they know it's what Dad wants to do," Jon said. "But when we're fishing in rivers, they really do prefer the fly rod. The best piece of advice I can give any parent is to help them but don't do everything for them, and above all don't push. As a father, I can't think of anything better than fly fishing with my two boys."

In general, the best way to get children interested in fly fishing is to follow their lead and offer gentle guidance. If you're already a fly fisher, resist the temptation to delve into every minute aspect of fly fishing while they're young, as Colin Archer learned. If you're learning together and want to attend a fly-fishing class with your youngster, I'd advise holding off on a full-blown multiple-day school, which often involves some classroom time, until your child is about ten years old. Instead, look for a short, one-hour casting lesson, and while you will enjoy the shared experience, don't criticize your child's progress. You've hired a professional for that, and it will go down much easier coming from someone else.

Regardless of your own skill level, here are some suggestions to help guarantee success.

1. Keep all fishing trips short at first. When your child's attention span begins to wander, pack up the fishing gear and move on to something that holds their interest.

2. When picking a fishing spot, find a place that also has good frog hunting or turtle chasing or minnow netting. These critters are usually found in shallow, weedy areas, so avoid deep water and quick drop-offs if possible. Don't forget a butterfly net!

3. Find a location with a playground or other kid-friendly attraction nearby so you can quickly move on to something else.

4. Pay attention to the way you dress your kids so they're comfortable. Slather on the sunscreen. Pack extra clothes in case they fall in, and take long pants and a sweatshirt in case it gets chilly on the water. Take child-friendly bug repellent. Make sure they wear hats and sunglasses to protect their eyes from hooks, especially when they first pick up a fly rod.

5. Take drinks and snacks. Pack a cooler. Kids get hungry and thirsty much quicker than adults.

6. Let kids fish with a fly rod any way they want. Put a worm or live grasshopper on the leader. Let them just dap for sunfish. Watch that they are at least safe with that fly whizzing around in the air, and then step away and let them make their own mistakes.

7. Never take kids fishing with only a fly rod. Kids need action, and your goal is to get them catching fish by any means. Pack a spinning rod or push-button rod, bobbers, and some bait.

Preteens and Teenagers—Make It Hands-On

You'll be happy to learn that from the youngest child to well into the teenage years, there seem to be few gender differences between boys and girls when it comes to fly fishing. The sport requires some hand-eye coordination but little upper-body strength, and professionals who teach children fly fishing have seen few variations in how boys and girls pick up the sport. This is not the case with adults, where real gender differences in how men and women learn and enjoy fly fishing are observed, but kids are kids when it comes to the natural world.

If you want to introduce a teenager to fly fishing, hopefully your child has already shown some interest in fishing with conventional gear. As Colin Archer learned, conventional gear should always be close at hand, even if you want your fishing trips to be pure fly-fishing trips. And you have to understand that some kids take to fishing and some don't, regardless of their parents' interests. You can find kids from completely urban households where no family members have ever shown an ounce of interest in fishing who just seem to decide, out of the blue, that they want to go fishing. On the other end of the spectrum, you'll find kids from fly-fishing families who want no part of it—but in those cases it's probably because they've been taught the wrong way in the past.

Evan Griggs, a fly fisher who is now in college studying environmental education, founded a high school fly-fishing club in inner-city Minneapolis and can vouch for the appeal fly fishing has for teenagers, even among those who did not have a parent or grandparent to take them fishing when they were younger. He saw that kids today were too busy with other activities to think about fishing, and it never even crossed their radar screens. He showed them videos like the *Trout Bum Diaries,* which are more like snowboarding movies than what we usually see on Saturday-morning fishing shows. Before he knew it, he had fifteen to twenty kids at every meeting, and soon they were out on the water casting, helping with river surveys, and even helping state crews with their electroshocking fish-sampling gear. Evan's secret was to get the kids immediately out in the field one way or another. "The worst thing you

If it's challenging enough, teenagers really take to fly fishing.

can do is drive three hours to a trout stream to fish for an hour and then come home," he told me. "I got them right out onto lakes in the city limits fishing for bass and sunfish."

Of course, learning from their peers is an ideal way for teenagers to learn fly fishing, but few places are lucky enough to have someone with the vision and organizational skills of Evan Griggs. But we can learn from his wisdom. "Get them out on the water. The more hands-on, the better," he advised me. "And don't preach to them. They've just spent six hours having teachers talk at them, and the last thing they need is another structured lesson."

Simon Perkins, who ran a kids' fly-fishing camp in Montana, has seen mistakes parents make in his experience as both a soccer coach and a fly-fishing instructor and guide, and he agrees. "The last thing a kid needs is to be lectured to or learn the way his parents learned," he tells me. "It's so natural for parents to pressure their kids, but it's a terrible thing to witness from the outside. My best advice to the parent of a teenager is to let someone else start them out. It could be a formal class or camp, but it can also be a grandparent, aunt, uncle, or fishing guide. I'll often guide a kid and parent together and I'll make a suggestion on the kid's technique, and often it immediately fixes the problem. The parent will say, 'That's exactly how I told him to do it,' but it's always better coming from someone other than the parent."

Embrace the Complexities with Older Kids

Unlike their younger siblings, teenagers thrive on the complexity of fly fishing. Caleb Parent, whose relationship with his father has blossomed since they both learned to fly fish together, feels it helps him deal with the immense pressures looming over today's teenagers. Even though Caleb lives in northern Vermont, no high school today is a Norman Rockwell painting. "I like the freedom of it," he told me. "I like to be on my own. I don't like the commitment of high school sports. When I'm out there fly fishing, my mind and body are so involved, I can't think about homework and grades. It's a good stress reliever, it's a healthy outdoor thing, and it's good exercise."

He likes fly fishing as opposed to conventional fishing because it's more involved, more hands-on. He loves the complexity of the sport. "You're not just sitting there. You're casting, reading the water, picking out the right fly. It's just more fun. And although it's a good bonding experience with my dad and a good self-bonding experience and helps me deal with family and emotional issues, I still get frustrated. I get my leader tangled, or I go out multiple times and get skunked. But it's the great days that keep me coming back."

If you have any doubt about the appeal of complexity to teenagers, look over the shoulder of a teen playing a computer game. Their minds thrive on solving complex puzzles, and rather than complaining about how much time they spend on the computer, it's our duty as parents to gently guide them into something that provides an equal degree of problem solving and complexity, but completely removed from any electronic device. Fly fishing does fit the bill.

In teaching teenagers, Simon Perkins sees the importance of introducing the complex aspects of fly fishing and then letting kids approach the sport from whatever angle they want. "Let kids connect to fly fishing in the way they want to connect," he stresses. "It may not be the way you, the parent, wants to connect. Some kids get turned on by casting, some love fly tying, some like studying aquatic insects, some prefer rowing a drift boat. That's fine. Watching kids learn fly fishing, I've also noticed that all older kids have their own way of learning. Some want to watch and mimic. Others want just a few basics and then want to hack around on their own. It's important to know, as a parent or instructor, when to step back."

I asked Simon if he ever had any kids in his fly-fishing camp for whom fly fishing just didn't take. "No," he said, "I've never seen it not take at least to some degree. The hardest case we ever had was a kid with severe ADHD. He started when he was twelve, and he was the worst at focusing we'd ever seen. At first I thought he was totally hopeless, but he came back four years in a row. We finally realized he had to learn at his own pace—he needed breaks and he needed to just skip rocks some days. I know that a parent would have been totally frustrated with him, but eventually he really got into turning over rocks and looking for bugs and became a decent fly fisher. He'll always be terrible at casting, but he's a decent angler now."

Today's teenagers have peers as fly-fishing role models, unlike kids in past generations. What was once the province of old guys smoking pipes and drinking scotch has been discovered by the ski and snowboard crowd, particularly in the Rocky Mountains. In the winter you'll often find fly fishing and snow sports coexisting in the same areas. Every ski resort in Colorado has a trout stream nearby, so naturally some of the ski bums in the area, who were already outdoors-inclined, discovered something fun to do when snow conditions weren't perfect, realizing that fly fishing requires more mental stimulation than running or mountain biking. And they made fishing movies that mimicked the high energy of skiing and snowboarding films, with fly fishers traveling to places like Mongolia and living in yurts, or fishing their way across the United States in a fashion that would make Hunter S. Thompson smile.

Fly fishing to this crowd is a physical, exotic, and even extreme sport. Film tours developed, along with the inevitable profanity but also with a fresh new take on fly fishing, attempting to describe the adrenaline rush of the sport as opposed to the serenity and contemplation that fly-fishing books and early videos portrayed. YouTube hosts thousands of short fly-fishing videos, with the quality spectrum inevitably ranging from horrible to gorgeously artistic, most of them with background music by indie rock bands and with few of the people on camera over the age of thirty.

Not all the films coming out of this renaissance have been home-movie quality. Fly-fishing movies by such brilliant filmmakers as Felt Soul Media have won film festival awards across the United States and Canada, and they are as artfully produced and as visually attractive as any modern documentaries. And filmmakers have given back to the resource. Felt Soul's *Red Gold* was a stunning, crafty rail against a monster gold mine planned for the Alaskan wilderness, and did more for raising awareness about the fight against Pebble Mine than any other form of media.

If you have a teenager you'd like to interest in fly fishing, I can think of nothing better than renting a copy of one of Felt Soul's fly-fishing films, like *Running Down the Man, The Hatch,* or *Eastern Rises.* They'll take you and your child from Colorado to Baja to Kamchatka, and your teenager will see fly fishing in a whole new light, from their own generation's perspective. The personalities in the films aren't teenagers, but the excitement level and production techniques are more in tune with music videos than *A River Runs Through It.* And don't rule out the value of fly-fishing videos on YouTube and similar crowd-sourced media venues, in terms of both entertainment and education. Granted, the educational value of many YouTube fly-fishing videos is a crapshoot, but many of the twenty-something fly fishers I know learned most of their fly fishing from YouTube.

Sometimes the Best Route to Fly Fishing Is through Fly Tying

The gateway drug to fly fishing for many kids has been fly tying. Kids often have time on their hands, they can't go off and fish anytime they want because of transportation restrictions, and they love to create stuff with their hands. Some kids who have absolutely no interest in fishing at all get turned onto fly tying. I've spent time in kids' cancer wards and summer camps for children with chronic illnesses, places like the Hole in the Wall Camps, and believe me, once you dump a pile of feathers and chenille and rubber legs on a table, it's hard to hold the kids back. Even those kids who couldn't fish or didn't even want to fish would get into fly tying, and flies would be proudly displayed on ball caps and even adorned earrings that some of the girls made.

Kids can also learn fly tying at a much earlier age than fly fishing. My son was tying decent flies when he was four years old. At that time he had very little interest in fishing in general and was years away from any desire to fish with a fly rod, but he would spend hours at his fly-tying vise, which was the only thing that kept him focused at that age. There is no strength, no gross motor skills, and really very little complex fine motor skill required for fly tying. It's far easier than learning to button a shirt or tie shoelaces.

Even kids who don't have much interest in fishing are fascinated with fly tying. My son was inventing his own creations at age four with very little encouragement from Dad.

When Evan Griggs taught his high school fly-fishing classes, he found that the girls were more interested in fly tying, at least at first, so tying is also a way to get older kids to embrace the sport, both boys and girls. If you don't tie yourself, older kids are quite capable of getting started on their own with a good basic book, but both young children and teenagers benefit from watching fly-tying videos. There are many thousands of fly-tying videos all over the web, both on YouTube and on various independent fly-tying blogs and websites. And don't fight it—that's the way we learn in today's world.

The best way to get kids started in fly tying is to buy your child a good basic kit. It will have a vise to hold the hook and the basic tools like a bobbin, dubbing needle, hackle pliers, and fine scissors. You can get fly-tying kits for a little as $20, but I'd advise you to spend somewhere around $100 to $150 if you're sure they'll enjoy it. The tools will be of better quality, the materials will likely be labeled so they can identify them, and the more expensive kits come with a better book or instruction manual, and sometimes a DVD. For the price of a big LEGO set or a portable video game controller, you can begin your child on an adventure that can be enjoyed for a lifetime. And once they begin creating these wild imitations of nature, the next step will be a desire to catch fish on them.

The best fly for anyone to begin with is a Woolly Bugger. It catches nearly anything, anyone can learn to tie one in an hour, and the materials are cheap and easily obtained; in fact, you can buy the chenille, fluffy marabou feathers, and saddle hackles in craft stores or in the craft departments of big-box stores. Marabou feathers are the fluffy feathers often used to make feather boas, and saddle hackles are the long, skinny chicken feathers used to adorn hats and jewelry. Cotton chenille in a small diameter might be the most difficult material to find in a craft store, but fine-diameter pipe cleaners work in a pinch.

Most fly tiers work with the hook clamped in the vise with the point showing, because it allows them more working room. However, for small children starting out, I always like to hide the point of the hook inside the jaws of the vise, which keeps little kids from poking themselves and from catching the thread on the point and breaking it. Other than that, dump a pile of materials on a table or desk and let your kid go crazy, with his or her imagination running wild. As with fishing, don't try to supervise and force them to tie standard patterns at first. Even if you already tie flies yourself, perhaps just show them how to use the bobbin, how to begin the thread on the hook and half-hitch the thread at the end, and how to wind materials, then walk away and let them have fun.

Parents and Children—The Dynamic Is Not Always What You Think

As you saw with my friends Jane and Ronan Cooke, fly fishing is not always a father-teaching-son activity, as it was perhaps in the past. Gender and age boundaries have blurred with regard to many aspects of life, and fly fishing is no different. And it's not always the parent that teaches the child. In the past few years, I've watched as local kids, children of my good friends, have become passionate about fly fishing when their parents were indifferent. For most of these kids, fishing was always an activity they enjoyed, but they became bored by the mechanical nature of conventional fishing.

Sam Mosheim is one of those kids. His father, Dan, is a good friend who makes custom furniture, and Sam is following in his father's footsteps as an artisan, preferring to work in wrought iron instead of wood. I've known Sam since he was a toddler, and never once did I hear him say anything about fly fishing until a few years ago, when his mother asked me to sign one of my basic fly-fishing books for him. Sam had gone crazy for fly fishing, and the culmination of that passion was a fly-fishing trip to Montana with his dad, who I know would pick up a fly rod every few years for an evening on a local stream and then put it away. But a full week of fly fishing is a sea change, and I am sure the beginning of a wonderful shared passion that was really passed down from a son to a father.

And sometimes parents and children learn together. Dan Parent is an EMT in northern Vermont and had always fished with his two sons and daughter, but neither his parents nor his grandparents had ever fished with a fly rod. The family always fished with spinning rods, even for trout. Dan had more shared interests with his older son, Ethan, than he had with Caleb, his younger son, as Dan and Ethan both enjoyed studying military history and flying radio-controlled planes, which didn't interest Caleb. One day before fishing, Caleb said, "Dad, why don't we try those old fly rods we have hanging in the garage?" They tried the fly rods, but without any instruction it was pretty frustrating, so they hired a guide to show them some casting and fishing techniques. Both Dan and Caleb soon realized that they were wild about fly fishing because it was more challenging and more complex, but also relaxing at the same time. "It was my first real strong connection with Caleb as a teenager," Dan said, and they are now inseparable fishing buddies.

Kids also become the teacher. Matt Wormell became the teacher for both of his parents, as told in this warm and inspiring post on his dad Dean's blog, but written by his mom, Valerie.

Dan and Caleb Parent discovered fly fishing together and found it a great way to get closer.

For years, we have vacationed in a quiet, Maine, mountain town. The agenda was always the same—a canoe trip on the Androscoggin, climbing a White Mountain 4,000 footer, fishing mountain lakes and streams and an evening of laser tag, provided the family with a sense of security and relaxation. Our son, Matt, was about to enter his senior year of high school, and we wanted one spectacular family vacation, choosing Rocky Mountain National Park in Colorado. Colorado offered some of the country's finest fly-fishing opportunities.

I grew up a bait chucker, fishing for perch in a 16-foot Lyman on Lake Erie. For four years, I lived on a trout stream in Meshoppen, Pennsylvania, and would take my spinning rod to the water, catching trout and suckers. I put the rod away after an unexpected encounter with a copperhead. On one of our early vacations in Maine, I decided to bring my spinning rod and show my rambunctious son the joy of fishing. After the first bluegill, my son was hooked. Fishing replaced dinosaurs as his universe.

When Matt was in grade school, we had a deal—get the homework done and we'll go fishing after dinner. The little pond down the street was full of bass and it became routine. Over the years, Matt has become an accomplished bass fisherman. Sometimes, I would join him, dog leash in one hand and fishing rod in the other.

I don't know how Matt became aware of the sport of fly fishing, but one day he asked me to take him to a store to buy a $60 fly fishing rod and reel combo. He practiced casting in the front yard and soon started catching bass on the fly. For Christmas, he was bound and determined to buy the same fly rod/reel combo for his dad and walked over fifty dogs to earn the money. Soon, father and son were taking float trips and weekend excursions throughout New England, fishing for rainbow, brooks and browns.

When you enjoy something, you have to share it with the ones you love, and that is how I learned to fly fish. Matt was my instructor. He had such skill and made the sport look effortless and elegant. Matt could easily have been the casting double for the movie, A River Runs Through It. *As a child, he didn't always have the patience to stay with me and correct my flaws, but would go off to fish on his own. As soon as I got a wind knot or tangled in a tree, he was gone. I accompanied my guys on several trips and never landed a fish. Matt was frustrated with me, but never stopped asking me to go.*

By the time we traveled to Colorado, Matt was a young man. Late one afternoon, fishing Arapaho Creek, Matt set his rod down and came over to sit near me. He had caught his fish for the day and wanted to give me a few words of encouragement. As usual, I hadn't caught anything. He suggested a Goddard Caddis and roll casting into the side of a pool. Fish on! I screamed. Matt ran for the net and waded into the water to make sure the fish didn't get away. It was nice-sized rainbow. My first trout on a fly. I don't know who had the bigger smile, me or Matt.

Even if your child is a novice fly fisher and you're more experienced, don't be surprised if your kid out-fishes you. Jim Hickey, a veteran guide who hosts many families on guided trips in Wyoming and Montana, has observed that kids, because they have laser-like focus and fewer distractions in their lives, keep their fly in the water more. Kids aren't as afraid to look silly as their parents are, and they seldom let their egos get in the way. As a result, they concentrate on catching fish and nothing else—and they get the job done.

As Jane Cooke found, fly fishing with kids isn't always a total family experience with both parents participating. And that's OK. Jon Luke's wife loves fly fishing, but when he goes fishing with his boys, she's very happy to stay home and have the house to herself. When they take family camping trips, everyone fly fishes, but it's natural and healthy for one parent to be the primary fly-fishing pal.

Your child or grandchild or nephew or niece just may not take to fly fishing, but I've given you the best advice I know to encourage the interest. Stand back, be patient, and let them discover the sport for themselves, with gentle guidance here and there. Let them observe your passion but don't let your passion overwhelm them, and remember that kids approach fly fishing from different angles and may learn to enjoy different aspects than you do. If it does take, just be thankful you have the best fishing buddy in the universe.

Chapter 6

Couples and Fly Fishing

Adults have more interests, biases, and distractions than kids. They are harder to teach and harder to get to try new skills that they might not grasp at first. Unlike most kids, adults *are* afraid of making mistakes in front of other people. And in order to have your husband or wife or brother-in-law enjoy fly fishing with you, they have to first enjoy fishing, period. Some people just have no interest in fishing, and if the person you want to introduce to fly fishing is cool to the idea of fishing in general, there may be little you can do to share your passion with them.

Fly fishing is primarily a male-dominated sport, but not always. Molly Seminek has been fly fishing since she was fifteen, when she returned from a rock concert with her sister and found, lying on her bed, her father's bamboo rod, a vest, a creel, and a pair of waders. Her dad simply said, "It's time we go fly fishing together," and for the rest of her teenage years she and her dad took a big fishing trip every summer in the Rocky Mountains. Molly became a fly-fishing junkie when she left home, and spent weeks on end living in a hammock on the Green River in Utah, learning from other anglers and from guides. She is now a Certified Master Fly Casting Instructor with the Federation of Fly Fishers and for the past eleven years has run her own fly-fishing guiding and teaching business, Tie the Knot Fly Fishing, based in Livingston, Montana.

But her husband, Rich, does not fly fish and has no interest in it. He enjoys being on the river with Molly and loves rowing a drift boat, but he could care less about catching fish. He's the dean of the College of Business at Montana State University and author of ten books on economics, and he

Molly Seminek with a brown trout from her beloved Yellowstone River.

Many women are intimidated by fly fishing, which was historically male-dominated, and are more comfortable taking lessons with a female buddy.

enjoys golf and baseball and is an excellent fly caster—he just doesn't like fishing. Like many happy couples who don't share the same passion for fly fishing, Molly and Rich have come to terms with the notion that there are activities they enjoy together and activities they enjoy apart. You may have to face this fact with your spouse.

When One Spouse Already Fishes

Let's face it—fly-fishing participation is about 80 percent male, so when we talk about getting a spouse interested in fly fishing, it's almost always the husband trying to get his wife to try the sport. The question is usually, "How do I get my wife interested in fly fishing enough so that we can enjoy it together?" In my thirty-five years teaching fly fishing and advising fly fishers, I have never once had a wife ask, "How do I get my husband into fly fishing?" It may happen, and by reading further you'll probably get some ideas, but I'm sticking to the more realistic and practical scenario.

Your first step should be to take your wife on a fishing trip, if she hasn't joined you on one already, but it must be the right trip. Invite her

If you learn fly casting with your spouse, it might be a good idea to stay out of earshot of each other.

as a non-fishing companion—don't try to teach her yourself because, unless you are the one husband in twenty who can teach his wife, this trip should only be to let her see what it's like. Don't invite your wife on a steelhead fishing trip in December when she has to shiver on the bank while you spend endless hours trying to get the one tug that winter steelheaders dream of and are perfectly capable of waiting days for. Take her on a trip to a gorgeous trout stream on a sunny day in June, when the water sparkles and it's the rare person who wouldn't just love to get into the water and feel it around her legs. If she likes to hike, take her on a trip into a remote canyon. If she doesn't like to hike, find a favorite spot close to the road where she can stay within her comfort zone. Look for a nice place where she can sit on the bank and watch.

It's very important that this first trip be a short one. After an hour or so, watching someone fly fishing is about as stimulating as watching an elementary school talent show when you don't have a kid participating. Plan to fish for an hour, then take a hike together or drive around in the mountains to take pictures or look at wildlife. Find a fishing spot near some shops she might like or a museum that may interest her, and either have a nice picnic on the water or take her to a wonderful restaurant.

If she expresses an interest in learning to fly fish, send her to school. You may be able to teach her yourself using the tips in this book, especially if you're a great teacher with a wealth of patience, but if you want to play the percentages, take my advice. If you're already a fly fisher, don't take the school yourself—in fact, stay as far away as possible. The last thing your wife needs is you hovering over her, contradicting the advice she gets from her instructor. Women enjoy learning with other women and are often intimidated by this male-dominated sport, so it really helps if she can go to a school or casting clinic with a female friend or family member. The best school for them to attend is one of the special women's-only schools offered by many fly shops, and it's worth spending a little more time and money finding one. There are also women's-only fly-fishing clubs and guide services run by women that not only teach but also run special fishing trips only for women, which after a school might really get your wife started on a positive note. This is an investment in a fishing partner as well as a life partner, so don't try to do it on the cheap.

Molly Seminek, after teaching and fishing with over 3,000 women, has developed a list of ten points for guides to consider when working with women, but these are also wonderfully valid points for any husband planning on fishing with his wife, so I've modified her list slightly to apply to husbands and wives.

1. Women can be hard on themselves. Give them small tasks to improve their self-confidence before overwhelming them with the minutiae of fly fishing.

2. Men dive right in and make mistakes in fly fishing without giving it a second thought. Women enjoy instruction and need a sense of confidence in their skills before they go out on the water. Give a woman the time to feel comfortable with casting and wading before the first serious fishing trip.

3. Women are more concerned about safety and wading. Don't wade into deep water and expect her to follow. Keep the water below her knees until she develops confidence, and buy her a wading staff. Stress that the wading will get easier as she develops her balance and confidence.

4. Women are concerned about releasing fish safely. Teach her how to release fish with minimal handling before that first trip. (Molly has even encountered women who intentionally try not to catch fish because of a concern with releasing them.)

5. Women enjoy the history, beauty, and ecology of rivers. Take her to spectacular places, study the history of the area so you can share it with her, and show her some of the critters that live under rocks before you start. Don't make it an entomology class—stress the abundance and the relationships between the bugs and the fish, but don't go into such detail that it becomes a lesson instead of an experience.

6. Provide a healthy lunch with choices. You make the lunch and you know what she likes. Don't expect her to survive on beef jerky for ten hours like you do.

7. Laugh as much as you can—keep it fun. Women are more concerned about making mistakes on the water than men. Make sure she knows that even experts get hung up in trees.

8. Adjust the time spent on the water. Most men like to stay on the water from dawn to dusk. Most women don't. Take breaks frequently, and make sure you take a long break for lunch. Read her signals and when she has had enough, quit. Save those marathon fishing trips for when you go by yourself or with the boys.

9. Women usually are more social on the water and like to fish closer together than men. Don't disappear around the corner as soon as you hit the water.

10. When fishing in a drift boat, make sure you don't keep your wife in the bow all day. The bow is the better position in a boat, but don't keep her there just because you want her to be successful. She doesn't want you and your guide watching her all day long.

Molly Seminek notes that wader fit is critical for women—don't get them too small, so there is room for lots of movement.

Spouses Learning Together

If neither spouse has fly fished before, taking fly-fishing classes together is a good idea, at least according to the couples I've met over the years who began fly fishing later in life. With both starting on the same level, the tendency of one spouse to criticize the other is minimized, and the shared experience of learning together is often valuable. You can begin with a formal school with classes lasting over a number of days, or you can both just take short fly-casting lessons and learn beyond the basics on your own. I

A fly-fishing trip together can be a wonderful vacation enjoying a shared passion.

do recommend that you at least take casting lessons, however, as trying to learn fly casting on your own is a tedious process, and most adults today just don't have the time and patience for beginning from scratch.

Don and Norma Haynes began fly fishing together after their son grew up and left them as empty nesters. They both took a four-hour introductory course from a local fly shop, and after the class Norma caught three wild brown trout on the Gunpowder River in suburban Maryland near their home. She then became the one who initiated all their fishing trips. Since that first experience Norma has arranged fishing trips for them in Colorado, Virginia, and Pennsylvania, as well as frequent trips to the Gunpowder. There is nothing better for getting a spouse as a fishing partner than instant success, so don't overlook this important point. Catch fish first. Everyone needs a little triumph for confidence.

Bob and Teresa Eastway had both fished occasionally throughout their lives but had never fished together. They have busy, stressful lives, Bob as a cardiologist and Teresa as a registered nurse in an eye surgery center. They both golfed, but it was not something they could enjoy together. Not being a golfer, I didn't quite understand this until Bob told me that most men and women don't play golf together. "There can be so much of a difference in the skill level between men and women," he told me, "because there is a difference in strength and thus even in the courses men and women play. I belong to a tournament course, which is too tough for Teresa, but her courses aren't much of a challenge and thus not much fun for me."

They wanted to do something together, so they tried fly fishing. They took a course from Truel Meyers, a seasoned instructor, at the Ocean Reef Club in Florida and soon became passionate about fly fishing. "Not only is it something we share," said Bob, "but now when we travel, we travel together because we're always looking for new fly-fishing trips to explore. Besides that, I find that fly fishing is much better stress reduction, especially if you're competitive like I am. Sure, I get a bit frustrated when I miss a fish, but believe me, it's nothing like the frustration you encounter in golf! I thought I'd miss golf, but honestly I don't miss it at all."

Bob and Teresa continue to take refresher casting lessons from Truel Meyers, and they've even taken fly-tying classes together. And they don't just take exotic trips as a couple—they enjoy fishing for trout on local streams, and they've even fished for winter steelhead together. As Bob said, "It's so easy to plan vacations now because we both want to do the same thing, and we've met some wonderful people on fly-fishing trips. It gives you a chance to reinvent your soul with someone you enjoy being with."

Couples Fishing Together

The most crucial part of fly fishing as a couple is the difference in expectations about what a day of fly fishing will entail. As Teresa Eastway told me, "When we fish with a guide in a drift boat, I don't mind fishing all day because we're committed. And I can sit back and relax. When we go fishing on a local trout stream, I'm ready to go before Bob. Bob can keep going all day, but not me." Gauge the length of your days as a couple, not as one person fishing alone. Agree on a time spent on the water and be flexible. Both of you should be willing to compromise a bit to make it a satisfying experience all around.

Some couples like to fish in sight of each other, but not all do. Don and Norma Haynes usually go their separate ways on a trout stream.

It's a good idea to carry a net when fishing with a novice, as it will prevent a fish's struggling when one is landed.

They cherish fly fishing as "something we can do together and share, but we can still have our solitude." Norma is totally indifferent to flies and gadgets and different techniques and is just happy to be on a river, so when her gear or fly selection needs a tune-up, she calls Don on the two-way radios they both have and he comes to help. It's interesting that Bob and Teresa Eastway use the same approach to keep in touch while river fishing.

Because men seem to enjoy the gear associated with fly fishing more than women, sometimes they overemphasize the importance of having a vest full of gadgets, perhaps even trying to justify all the money they've spent over the years once their spouse sees how much they've accumulated. Don't overload your spouse with a vest full of leader gauges, knot-tying tools, stream thermometers, fly floatants, and multiple fly boxes. All these trappings are clumsy, heavy, and intimidating. Women in particular don't always enjoy fishing vests because they seldom fit properly. Consider a small sling bag or waist pack with just the bare essentials for a woman starting out in fly fishing. As she finds a real need for gadgets she can add them later, but don't scare her off in the beginning.

Molly Seminek also finds that wader fit is critical for women, and that when most women try on waders for the first time, they want to buy a pair that is too small. Fly shop owners aren't much help, either, because they often ignore the carefully designed size charts put out by manufacturers. Women should understand that they need to be able to kneel down and climb up a steep bank in waders, and if the waders are too tight, they won't allow the freedom of movement that's required.

Because women are more concerned with struggling fish than men, two important considerations will help make releasing fish easier on everyone. First, carry a net. A fish can be handled and photographed with much less struggling when it's confined safely to a net instead of flopping around in the water. A net with a wide, shallow, flat net bag instead of a deep, cone-shaped bag makes admiring and photographing fish much easier. The second point is to always crimp barbs on flies before fishing. Flies without barbs slip right out of a fish with your fingers, and even with fish that are hooked deeply, a barbless fly can be quickly backed out with a pair of forceps without a lot of handling.

Once you begin to fish together, bear in mind that a fishing trip with your spouse will not be an eight-hour marathon. The more gung-ho, experienced partner should save those kinds of trips for solo expeditions or trips with other fanatic anglers. It's no fun for either person when one wants to quit and the other wants to keep going. Couples fishing trips should be about more than just fishing. Plan for a long and elegant streamside lunch, or spend half the day taking pictures in a scenic area. Bring along a canoe or a pair of kayaks and spend part of the day just enjoying the feeling of gliding across the surface of a calm lake.

One aspect of fishing together should be self-evident, but based on what I hear from guides like Jim Hickey, the urge to compete is not always checked at the boat ramp. In any couple one is typically more competitive than the other, and a spouse should not try to compete, nor should the more competitive spouse hold back or try to give his or her partner the best spot or the most attention from the guide. One way of accomplishing this is to withstand the urge to count or measure fish. I know it's hard because we live in a competitive society that likes to measure everything, but I can assure you that if you don't count fish and don't bother to measure the biggest fish, you will both return from a day of fly fishing with much more of an experience than a scorecard can offer.

Age Doesn't Matter

A common scenario of couples learning to fly fish together is a pair of empty nesters looking for something active and outdoors to do together now that the kids are gone. But with fly fishing becoming more interesting to young people in the twenty-first century, that isn't always the case. Tyler Adkins and Chrissy Penn were in their early twenties when they began to fly fish together. Tyler had been a lifelong fly fisher, but although Chrissy had fished when she was young, she had never held a fly rod. Bucking the odds, Tyler taught Chrissy how to cast and took her to a nearby lake to catch sunfish on a fly rod.

All was well until they went trout fishing together. Then it all fell apart. Tyler wanted to fish right away, Chrissy took twice as long as he did to get geared up, and Tyler promptly disappeared around the bend.

Chrissy was mystified by the complexities of trout fishing, especially reading the water and deciding which fly to tie on. She wanted to try everything by herself first, but if she struggled, she wanted Tyler close by so he could help her with knots or picking the right fly. Tyler wanted a fishing buddy like his male fishing buddies—get to the river, fish apart for a few hours, then get back together and compare notes.

Tyler Adkins and Chrissy Penn prove that not all fly-fishing couples are empty nesters.

So despite their youth, they experienced the same issues most couples encounter. He is more interested in fishing from dawn to dusk and going off by himself; she's happier if he is within sight, and she may want to quit after a half day and do something else. "I did enjoy fishing by myself one day," she told me, "when we were carp fishing on a river. I went to the other side of an island and hooked a really nice fish and was very proud of myself, but then there was no one to share my triumph with and I wished Tyler had been there."

They've learned to split the difference in the length of their trips, and they enjoy fishing from a canoe, when they can be together and one can paddle while the other fishes. Chrissy offers some words of advice for young couples, but really for couples of any age, learning to fish together:

- Don't begin fly fishing with trout fishing. If I had started out trout fishing, I would have been frustrated and would probably have given up.

- If you learn together, stay separated. Don't be within earshot; that way you can't criticize each other.

- Don't just use one instructor. Take a school with multiple instructors or get follow-up lessons. It sometimes takes a number of different approaches before some aspect of casting really clicks.

- Let me struggle with something for ten minutes, and if I don't get it by then, you can help me.

- Don't always give your girlfriend or spouse the best hole or the best position in the boat. It puts too much pressure on her.

- Take a trip and do some kind of fly fishing that the more experienced partner has not done before. Tyler and I went to South Carolina to try for redfish on a fly, and it was encouraging for me to see him struggling with something as much as I was for a change.

Throughout our conversation Tyler quietly nodded to what Chrissy said, and when she finished, I asked him if he had anything to add to her suggestions. His only suggestion was succinct and appropriate: "Learn when to keep your mouth shut."

And If It Doesn't Take . . .

You should be prepared for your partner to dislike fly fishing or only participate because it's what you want. Do you really want to drag someone along who is not having as good a time as you are, or who hates the idea of putting on waders or stepping into a drift boat? People like Molly Seminek and Jane Cooke have learned to coexist happily with spouses who don't fish. Your dream of getting the entire family together for a fly-fishing trip could turn into a trip with just you and one of your kids, or you and a parent or a cousin. Embrace the partners you have and learn to take trips that are strictly fishing-oriented with them, and plan other trips for the entire family that have only minimal fly fishing.

Before my wife, Robin, took up fly fishing and when my son, Brett, was too young to fish, I learned to satisfy my craving and still participate in family activities by fishing the odd hours of the day. For instance, we'd take an annual trip to Cape Cod, where we would rent a house for a week. I'd make sure that the house was within walking distance of some decent fishing, and I would plan my fishing times either at dawn or after dark. Striped bass, like many other gamefish, feed actively at dawn and dusk, when their prey species become active and light levels are lower, so I probably got the best fishing of the day but at the same time was back to the house by breakfast and could enjoy the day with my family until well after dinner. Of course, you sacrifice some sleep when you follow this plan, but when on vacation, most of us don't have to be quite as alert as we need to be during our normal workweeks.

This kind of after-hours fishing also works out well for tropical salt-water species like snook, redfish, tarpon, and bonefish. Most bonefishers don't even realize that the best times for tailing fish are at dawn and dusk, because most lodges and guides follow a daylight schedule to allow for meals and for sight-fishing during the day. But if you plan a bonefishing trip, make sure that there are at least a few flats within walking distance of where you are staying that you can get to on foot or bicycle or rental car at dusk and especially at dawn. Dawn fishing is easier because you'll be sure not to miss any meals, and in places with lots of boat traffic during the day, bonefish feed heavily at dawn after the water has had the chance to settle down. The rest of the day you can spend walking on the beach, snorkeling, or kayaking with your family.

One bonefishing lodge that I frequent regularly is located on a highly developed beach lined for miles with resorts. Yet the best fishing I have there is when I get up a half hour before daylight and walk the beach look-ing for tailing bonefish. By getting up before the sun, I have even seen the elusive permit tailing at dawn right alongside docks that are busy with boat traffic the rest of the day.

During the summer, trout fishing at either end of the day also gives you the best fishing. We all know about the evening hatch, when bugs cover the water and fish lose their daytime caution because of lower light levels and increased amounts of light-shy insects. But fishing at first light can be equally productive, especially with nymphs and streamers. Again, people who spend most of their time on guided trips don't see this kind of fishing since guided trips typically began at 8 or 9 a.m. and last until 3 or 4 in the afternoon, because guides, like most of us, work an eight-hour day and need time to spend with their families or prepare for their trips the next day. But if you're on your own, don't pass up these fishy times when you can get in some great fishing and sacrifice very little of the time you spend with your family.

Chapter 7

More Complex Fishing Trips

Eventually you and your family will look for new challenges—bigger fish, majestic trout streams you've seen in magazines or on TV, or perhaps the excitement of fly fishing in the ocean. I don't recommend that you jump right from a local sunfish pond to a weeklong trip to an exotic destination, and by exotic I don't mean something you have to jump on a plane to do or spend thousands of dollars to try. Exotic could mean a car trip to a northern lake where big pike are the quarry instead of pan-size sunfish.

The desire to look for new species or fish new waters is natural to most people who enjoy fly fishing. Part of the pleasure we get out of this sport is the constant challenge to our natural curiosity and the desire to learn new techniques. In fly fishing you'll probably learn something new every time you string up your rod, and this won't change until the day you can't pick up your rod anymore. True experts in fly fishing don't ever consider themselves experts, because at a certain point they realize they'll never figure out half of the puzzles they're presented with every time their feet get wet.

I used to believe some kinds of fly-fishing trips should never be considered for family outings. Tarpon fishing in the Florida Keys, for instance—where the fish are huge, the fishing is intense and competitive, guides can be difficult and downright abusive, and less than ideal weather conditions can lead to many fishless days—wouldn't seem to be ready-made for families. But I mentioned this to my friend Captain Rick Ruoff, one of the most experienced tarpon guides in the Florida Keys, on a recent fishing trip, and he took exception to the idea.

Rick had a father-and-daughter charter one day, and the father spent the morning unsuccessfully trying to hook a tarpon while his ten-year-old daughter sat patiently in the boat, watching sharks and dolphins and rays. At midday the dad was frustrated and fatigued, and Rick suggested the man's daughter give it a try. "You mean she can do this?" the father asked. "Sure, with a quick casting lesson," Rick replied, and he soon had the daughter casting 30 feet of line. A school of big tarpon slid into view. Rick had the daughter throw to the lead fish, which promptly ate the fly and put on the usual explosion of water, with gills flaring and the manic airborne ballet so typical of tarpon. Luckily the fish threw the hook because it was doubtful the little girl could have played and landed it. But she couldn't stop talking about how exciting it was and surely had some stories to tell her classmates when she returned home.

Winter steelhead fishing, with icy banks, the potential for frostbitten hands, and a very real prospect of an entire weekend spent without a single fish on the line, is another trip I wouldn't ordinarily recommend for a family. Yet Tim Daughton and Shawn Brillon, two friends and colleagues, regularly take their teenage sons steelhead fishing, and the boys anticipate the next trip as much as any other fun activity.

So although I have learned not to make assumptions about what constitutes a good venue for the next challenge on a family fly-fishing trip, I feel there are some trips that provide an extra measure of excitement and learning even while providing quick action and needing only a moderate amount of proficiency from novice fly fishers. Just bear in mind that anytime you venture beyond the always-there, always-eager world of small bass and sunfish, you're subject to the whims of weather and fish migration. No matter what you read or hear about, even the best trout stream in the world will serve up days when no one can catch fish, not even the local experts. The very unpredictability of fish, although frustrating at times, is what gives fishing its mystery and its appeal. If we didn't have to unlock the puzzle each time we stepped into the water, most of us would move on to something less predictable.

Suggestions for the First "Serious" Family Fishing Trip

What follows are suggestions for your first trip. They are not meant to be guides to catching certain species. Pick out the fishing that sounds appealing to you, and choose based on your travel budget and location. Then do some research by checking websites, books, and magazine articles on the venue you've chosen. In chapter 8 I'll go into more detail on how to pick a guide for a family trip, but the fishing trips described below can be approached successfully without a guide. Just do a little research first, which many anglers find is half the fun.

Stream Smallmouths

Smallmouth bass combine the allure of fishing in moving water with a fish that actually fights better than a trout of equal size, but doesn't fight so hard that the novice has a long, drawn-out battle on his or her hands. Smallmouths prefer rivers slightly warmer than what is optimum for trout, and thus are found closer to cities (where both development and the lower altitudes associated with most cities produce warmer temperatures) and also in the lower, downstream reaches of trout streams, where they are often ignored by anglers in search of the more glamorous trout species. Smallmouths are found from Maine to California, and down into southern rivers except for in the Deep South. They prefer clear, rocky waters, so they are often found in rivers that are a pleasure to wade or float in a canoe.

Stocked Trout Streams and Ponds

Freshly stocked trout have little fear of humans and will sometimes bite anything that looks even remotely edible. They are great for novices. Often streams that normally wouldn't support trout (perhaps because the water is too warm) are stocked by state or local governments or private fish and game clubs in early spring and fall, where the trout are expected to be caught within a few weeks, before succumbing to marginal water conditions. States as far south as South Carolina, Texas, and Arizona stock suburban streams, so this is not just a fishery you'll find in what is typically known as trout country.

Smallmouth bass are eager to take flies and are spectacular fighters. In most places they are more abundant and easier to find than trout.

Trout stocked in many streams don't last more than a month before succumbing to predators or fishing pressure, largely because the wariness inherent in wild, naturally reproduced trout has been bred out of them. Those fish that do survive beyond a month have learned to become wary, and thus are almost as difficult to catch as wild trout. So finding a fishing spot for the family where trout are easy to catch is a matter of checking the stocking records, which are found on state websites or published in local papers. Some waters, like the famous Trout Parks in Missouri, are stocked weekly to provide easy fishing throughout the season. Other stocked waters, especially those in southern states, are stocked only in the colder months.

Freshly stocked trout are easily caught on small black Woolly Bugger streamers stripped through the water. If that proven method fails to work, a large brown nymph or beetle fly will suggest the fish pellets fed to trout in hatcheries, attracting stocked trout and making them strike.

Wild Trout Streams

Most would-be fly fishers associate fly fishing with wild trout. Wild trout, those bred in nature instead of a hatchery tank, are the essence of wildness that many of us seek when we pick up a fly rod. Wild trout are warier and thus more of a challenge, but they also fight harder and their colors are more brilliant than stocked trout. However, I take issue with the idea that hatchery trout don't taste as good as wild trout. Hatchery trout are invariably raised in cold springwater with a high-protein diet that consists mostly of fish meal, not liver pellets as is commonly suggested. I've found hatchery trout as tasty as any wild trout, although I think the pure suggestion of wild brook trout fried in butter along the banks of a mountain stream in an old cast-iron pan makes them taste better. Blindfolded, I doubt if I could taste the difference between a wild and hatchery fish.

If you want to take your family fishing for wild trout, choose your location carefully. The farther you go from civilization, the easier the fish will be to catch. Don't expect to park at the first pull-off on the Missouri River in Montana, where each pool sees scores of anglers and hundreds of flies per day, and expect to have some family fun. In other words, avoid famous trout streams with their associated high fishing pressure and smart fish. Smaller high-mountain streams or lakes will have much easier fishing. Sure, getting there will be tougher and you might have to backpack or horseback to reach these waters, but a family fly-fishing trip should be an adventure anyway.

In general, streams and lakes with brook trout, such as those in southern Canada and New England (especially Maine), and Rocky Mountain and West Coast rivers with cutthroat trout will offer easier fishing. Both of these species evolved in sterile, food-limited environments and are less picky about what they eat, making them a lot more eager to come to the fly.

One of the best ways to get your family started on wild trout is with a wet fly swung in the current. Here, little fly or line manipulation is

Trout, whether stocked or wild, are what most people think of when they imagine fly fishing. Trout are wary and live in beautiful places, thus their allure.

needed, and all that's required is to get them to cast across the current—the force of the water does the rest, and because the fly swings on a tight line, fish often hook themselves. In fact, because their striking reflexes are slower than those of more experienced anglers, novices often hook a greater percentage of fish that take a swung fly.

You need the right kind of water for this type of fishing. Look for water with a uniform flow that is about the speed of a walk. Tails of pools and deeper riffles usually offer this kind of water. Heads of pools often have trickier currents, and the technique does not always work well in the slower water in the middle of a pool. But if the water is moving at that optimum speed of a walk (about 1 to 3 feet per second) and does not offer lots of swirly currents, the technique will be effective in those spots as well.

Using a 9-foot leader with a 4X or 5X tippet, attach a soft-hackled wet fly in size 14 or 16 to the end of the tippet. Any soft hackle should do, but the Partridge and Orange or Gold-Bead Hare's Ear versions are good places to start. Have your students cast directly across the current in slower water or at a slightly more downstream angle in faster water. Then just have them follow the progress of the fly downstream with the rod tip. Trout usually take the fly just as it begins to straighten and tighten at the end of the swing, but don't have your students cast as soon as the fly gets below them. Let the fly dangle in the current a bit, and then have them make a few strips back upstream, as fish sometimes follow the fly across and then eat it as it darts back upstream.

No one knows if this technique imitates an insect hatching or a small baitfish swinging against the current, but under the right conditions it is an effective, easy, and relaxing way to fish. It works best when the fish are active, which means water temperatures between 50 and 65 degrees. If the water is fast or deeper than 2 feet, you might also have your students make a quick mend upstream as soon as the fly lands, to help sink the fly and slow down its speed. It's also important to cover a lot of water. Have them begin with a very short cast, gradually lengthening line on each subsequent cast. After a dozen casts with no results, have them walk downstream 5 feet and repeat the process, so they are constantly covering new water.

One of the best times to fish this method is when caddisflies are hatching. Some species of caddis are very active swimmers in the pupa stage, so a fly moving across the current is realistic, and trout will be searching for flies that behave like the naturals. In fact, my friend John Packer of Avon, Colorado, a superb guide and fly shop owner, loves to have beginners in his drift boat when caddis are hatching. Both the pupae and adults are quite active on the water, and even when dry-fly fishing, a fly that drags across the current (ordinarily something to avoid when fishing dries) will draw strikes as well as a dry fly presented in the typical drag-free natural drift. You can't always coincide family fishing trips with a good caddis hatch, but if you can plan your trip for a time when caddis hatches are abundant (usually May and early June), your chances of success should be better.

Northern Pike

Northern pike are about as exotic a fish as you'll find in freshwater. With rows of needle-sharp teeth and the long, sleek body of a master predator, they lie in wait for hapless minnows and frogs to stumble into the wrong

Northern pike are big and nasty-looking. Kids love catching them, and so do adults.

neighborhood. My friend Jane Cooke, who lives and works in New York City, takes special fly-fishing trips with her twelve-year-old son, Ronan, every year. Even though they have fished in many places, Ronan's favorite spot to fish is Scott Lake in Canada for northern pike because he loves the way they slash at a fly.

If you decide to take your family for a pike trip, choose your waters carefully. When found in lakes in the United States, pike are easy on a fly rod only for a few weeks in the spring, because they retreat to cooler waters in late spring and summer. Better pike fishing is found in Alaska and Canada, where the water stays colder throughout the summer and fish can be caught on a fly in shallow water throughout the typical vacation season. Pike are also found in slow-moving, deeper rivers in the northern United States. Here they can be easier to take on a fly because the fish don't retreat to deeper water after early spring. However, this fishing is not as dependable as it is in waters north of the Canadian border.

Alaska for Salmon, Trout, and Pike

For most of us, Alaska is a long and expensive vacation, but if you have the time and disposable income, a family fly-fishing trip to Alaska is worth the effort. The scenery and wildlife-viewing are unlike any other place in North America, so even if the fishing is poor, it is a rare family that can't find something of interest. And the fishing is hardly ever poor. The number of fish in Alaska's rivers and lakes in the summer—combined with the unsophisticated willingness of species like rainbow trout, silver salmon, grayling, and northern pike to take streamers, nymphs, and egg flies fished on short, heavy leaders—makes for a high-volume fishing trip and action for everyone.

Beware that not all fishing in Alaska is a novice angler's paradise. Because of the vast wilderness and Alaska's limited road system, travel into remote areas is limited to float planes or long boat rides. With a population of well over 200,000 and over a 10 percent growth rate, Anchorage is hardly a backwater town, and rivers within driving distance of that city can, when salmon are running, look as crowded as New Jersey trout streams on opening day. To experience the best fishing and avoid crowd scenes near Anchorage and the well-traveled Trans-Alaska Highway, it's necessary to book a trip with a lodge or an outfitter that flies into a remote river and then floats for a few days to a week, camping along the way. Both options will offer the experience of a lifetime but with correspondingly steep prices.

Largemouth Bass

Thus far we've talked about fishing for small largemouth bass in local ponds and haven't introduced trying to catch bigger bass. But world-class fishing for largemouth bass can be found throughout the United States, from suburban water-supply reservoirs near San Diego to golf course ponds in Miami to farm ponds in Nebraska. Largemouth bass don't need

Largemouth bass are found almost everywhere and are lots of fun on a fly rod.

much to thrive and will grow to trophy sizes in places that can't even support trout, pike, or smallmouth bass.

Although the small bass you began with are always eager to take a fly, going after a more substantial fish takes some planning. Timing is important, both in terms of season and time of day. In big lakes the best time to fish for largemouths is in the spring, when fish are spawning and prowling the shallows, where they can be spotted and fished to with a fly rod. During the spawning season, anytime from late February in the South through late June in the North, largemouth bass will take a fly all day long, from first light through dark. Once the spawning season is over, the bigger bass retreat to deeper water during the day but come into the shallows in early morning and late evening to feed on baitfish, frogs, and larger insects like dragonflies.

In smaller golf course ponds, park ponds, and farm ponds, bass can't retreat to deeper water, but they may still be hidden and reluctant to feed in the middle of the day. However, dawn and dusk are another matter. There is a pond on a golf course near my house where fishing is frowned upon, but if I sneak in at dawn, before the grounds crew makes their rounds, I can catch surprisingly big largemouth bass (for Vermont anyway, up to 4 or 5 pounds) on poppers, which is way more exciting than catching 6-inch trout from our local streams. But that's just to show you that big bass can be found almost anywhere—I'm not suggesting that you pack up your family and make commando raids on local golf courses at the crack of dawn. Find a pond or lake somewhere where you can get permission to fish, and try it before the sun hits the water or boat traffic gets cranking.

Striped Bass and Bluefish

Saltwater fish are always more difficult for a family trip than freshwater species because most of them are constantly on the move, and a place that was teeming with fish one day can be barren the next—or even hours later. Tides, migration patterns, and prey abundance affect where saltwater fish live and feed, and ocean waters can be barren of fish for many square miles, even if the ecosystem is healthy and populations are not

Striped bass prefer shallow water, and small ones can be caught along almost any beach in the Northeast during the summer.

overfished. You need action and predictability for your first family trips, and saltwater fish don't always provide either.

Along the Atlantic coast, from Maine to North Carolina, striped bass and bluefish offer the most predictable fishing. June and July from Maine to Long Island, May and October from Long Island down through the coast of New Jersey, and April and November in the Chesapeake region and North Carolina are the best times to catch the biggest fish, but smaller juvenile stripers can be found all summer long throughout the range of both species. Striped bass are more likely than bluefish to be found farther upstream in estuaries and even small tidal creeks, but the best way to ensure a great family fishing trip is to fish for both species offshore, in tidal rips and offshore bars. For this you either have to hire a charter boat or use your own boat, but once these fish set up in their summer feeding grounds, they are as predictable as any saltwater fish can be, and the chances of having a fun and productive family trip are reasonable. Weather and wind always play a part, and it's rare to find a calm day anywhere within the range of striped bass and bluefish, so your schedule should remain flexible, as fishing with a fly rod is the easiest and most productive on calm days.

If you decide to book a charter boat, make sure that your family is the only party on the boat and that the captain specializes in fly fishing. Getting these fish on a fly is not the same as trolling for them with wire line, and it requires an experienced captain to find conditions just right for fly fishing.

Of course, you can also catch striped bass and bluefish from shore with your family, especially in the peak months mentioned earlier. Swimming beaches, jetties, and mouths of tidal creeks usually hold at least a small population of "schoolie" bass from a foot to 2 feet in length. Stripers especially love shallow water and are most active there at dawn and dusk. The best times are typically when you have the beginning of either an outgoing or incoming tide, but this varies with other local factors. Instead of trying to time the tide just right, it's easier to try to hit these spots at sunrise and sunset, regardless of the tides.

For any saltwater trip, make sure you pack a suitable spinning rod as a backup. Wind is nearly guaranteed on any saltwater fishing trip, and there will be times when all but the most die-hard fly fishers just can't deal with the wind. For most novices, anything more than 10 mph makes it tough; at 15 mph even experts have trouble; and once it gets past 20 mph, there are few fly fishers who won't pick up a spin rod. Don't forget that in these first expeditions it's all about catching fish, and nothing makes a fly fisher more enthusiastic than success, even if they have to catch some fish on a spinning rod.

Speckled (Sea) Trout and Ladyfish

From South Carolina through Texas, along the south Atlantic and then around the Gulf of Mexico, the most predictable fish is the speckled trout, or sea trout. These fish, popular with anglers of all ages, are invariably eager to bite and tend to stay in the same location from one day to the next. Look for them in channels adjacent to shallow water over grass beds, and around oyster bars. Most any streamer or popper, worked

Speckled trout, or sea trout, are easy to catch and very abundant in southern coastal waters.

quickly and aggressively, will interest these beautiful fish, and because they are a popular sport and food fish, states have set minimum sizes on how big they have to grow before you can keep them for the table. As a result, spots that teem with smaller trout are often ignored by local anglers—but the little ones are still lots of fun on a fly rod.

You may also find redfish in the same areas as sea trout. And while redfish are great fish on a fly rod, they are also more particular about what they eat and can be frustratingly wary, especially where fishing pressure is high. They are not as reliable a fish for a family outing as trout.

Ladyfish are another great species for a family fly-fishing trip, due to both their willingness to take a fly and the predictability of finding them. They range from North Carolina to the Caribbean and along the Gulf Coast, and are most often found at the mouths of deep channels and along the edges of bars in moving tidal current. Ladyfish eagerly take poppers and small streamers and are not wary in the slightest. Once hooked, they jump like miniature tarpon, which adds much to the fun of catching them. They are, in fact, often called the "poor man's tarpon,"

Ladyfish take flies readily and jump like tarpon. Not many people fish for them on purpose because they don't get very big, but they are fantastic on a fly rod.

although, unfortunately, a 20-inch specimen is considered a big one, and most are between 12 and 18 inches.

And Don't Forget Conventional Tackle

No matter what you do on your first serious fishing trip with the family, don't forget to take a conventional spinning rod (or push-button rod if you have younger children). Pack some worms, salmon eggs, or frozen shrimp and an assortment of effective spinning lures or bass baits. If the wind picks up or the fish go too deep or just plain aren't interested in a fly, you should have a Plan B to avoid disappointment. You may be a fly-fishing purist yourself, but don't force that mindset on your family unless they agree with it.

Family fishing trips are just that—*fishing* trips. Your spouse, parents, or kids probably don't care that much what kind of rod they have in their hands. At least not yet . . .

First Solo Attempts

Before you get to a lake or river and send your family out on their own, to help ensure success and prevent frustration, there are a number of things to watch for and to stress to them before they start. When you are actually faced with a body of water on your own, the complexities really start to add up. Many of the skills they learn will happen in due course, by making mistakes and figuring out how to correct them on their own, but there are a number of situations that always seem to confuse and frustrate first-time fly fishers. I've listed the most important ones, along with ways you can help beginners learn.

Dealing with Current

One of the first complexities novice anglers struggle with is current. They learn casting on a lake or pond, but then you take them to a trout stream and the water moves the fly line as soon as it hits the water. They're ready to make another cast, but suddenly the line and fly are pointed in another direction.

Changing Directions

The biggest mistake I see in most novice anglers is that they try to make a cast when the line and fly are 90 degrees away from the direction of the cast. Trying to cast a line straight out in front of you when the current has moved your line off to your left or right side will sweep the cast right through your body. This can result in a bad cast at best, and at worst can swat the fly into your shirt—or your anatomy. All anglers new to moving water should learn to face the fly line when making a cast and, when changing direction more than about 30 degrees, to make a false cast or two as they pivot their body.

Mending Line

Another essential technique when fishing in moving water is mending the line. You'll often cast over conflicting currents, and the most common situation is a fast current between you and where your fly lands. The faster current between you and the fly puts a belly in your fly line, which can do a number of things. If you are fishing a sinking fly, this belly in the line will pull your fly close to the surface, skimming it along the top too quickly, preventing it from sinking. When fishing a dry fly, this belly creates drag, which yanks the fly along the surface, making it look unnatural (most natural insects float serenely on the water and don't skim across the surface), usually resulting in a fish ignoring your fly.

Think of mending as a way of repositioning your fly line once your presentation has hit the water. It comes in handy in many situations, and I find that this is one skill that novice fly fishers typically have not learned before their first trip in a drift boat with a guide. The first thing a guide will tell you to do once your cast hits the water is to mend, and people who have taken a fly-casting class on a pond or on grass often have no idea what the guide is talking about.

Mending line is really simple. Raise the rod enough to break the surface tension on the line and then flip the rod tip in a semicircle (with the curved part of the semicircle pointing up) either upstream or downstream. That's all there is to it. The longer the line, the more you have to raise the rod tip and the longer the arc you have to make, but for short casts, just raising the rod a foot and flipping the line upstream is all you need to do. The best mends don't move the fly at all, so don't make your mends so aggressive that you move the fly out of position.

Gathering Line

Keeping the fly line tight to the tip of the rod is another issue I see when people first go from still water to moving water, and the problem arises when fishing directly upstream, as you often do with dry flies and nymphs and occasionally with streamers. When you cast upstream, the current brings the line toward you, and if you don't immediately get the line under control, slack line builds up under the rod tip. This slack line makes it almost impossible to set the hook, and it also makes picking up line for another cast iffy. When you raise the rod to begin another cast, all the slack has to be taken up before the rod starts to bend. Because the rod has to bend to build up enough energy to make a cast, the best way to make a cast is to begin the rod moving with tension on it. Slack line robs you of this tension.

The easy solution is to strip in line as the current brings it to you. Keeping the line pointed straight out of the rod tip ensures that picking up for another cast will efficiently bend the rod, and when a fish strikes, because of the direct connection, it takes very little effort to drive the fine wire of a fly hook into the fish's jaw. Strip line just as quickly as the current brings it to you—no slower and no faster. Don't strip so quickly that you move the fly, but strip quickly enough to gather up that slack that builds up under the rod tip.

Drag

If a feeding trout won't take your fly, it's probably because the fly is not moving naturally in the current. Trout often feed on helpless insects that are twitching and struggling in the surface film, not swimming across the surface like a speed skater. Dry flies and nymphs are most often fished "dead drift," which simply means that the fly moves just as fast as the current around it—no faster and no slower.

Mending line is one way to avoid drag, but there are better ways. One is to cast directly upstream so your fly line and the fly are always in the same current lane, and you just gather the slack line as the fly returns to you. But often you have to cast across currents, and mending often moves the fly too much and too late. An easier way to eliminate drag is to purposely cast a slack line—in other words, what looks like a "bad" cast. The coils of slack have to pay out before the line snatches the fly and drags it off target, and although an entire book could be written on ways to eliminate drag in dry-fly and nymph fishing, I'll give you a few ways to start.

The first is to purposely overpower your cast and end the cast higher than you normally would, making the line straighten above the water, snap back toward you, and land in soft coils. Another is to wiggle the tip of the rod as the line is descending to the water—after you complete the stop at the end of the forward cast, as you lower the rod to the water. Yet a third way is to make a reach cast, in which you make a mend in the line before the line hits the water.

This last technique requires a little more explanation. Imagine you are casting across a piece of fast current into slow current where trout are feeding. The current is moving from right to left. As you complete your forward cast, just before the line hits the water, reach the rod out and to the right in an exaggerated motion. This forms a cast with an upstream curve in it, and the curve has to invert before placing tension on your fly and dragging it. You may not get more than a few feet of drag-free drift with any of these techniques, but that's usually enough to fool a trout.

Dealing with Wind

You've learned to cast on a nice protected pond. In the real world, however, wind often rears its ugly head, particularly on big lakes, wide-open mountain rivers, and in nearly every saltwater environment. Fly fishing in the wind is more difficult, no question, because instead of firing a nice dense piece of plastic or metal through the air as you would when spin fishing, with fly fishing you're trying to maintain control of a long, air-resistant piece of string. There are ways to cheat the wind, and your family should know these tricks before you venture forward in a major fishing expedition.

Headwinds and Tailwinds

The wind in your face feels good when sailing, but it's no picnic when fly fishing. The best way to handle a headwind is to ease up on your back-cast (the wind will help you here, and if you overpower it, the wind may push the line down behind you) and make a more aggressive forward stroke. Don't make the mistake of reaching your arm out when casting into the wind—make an aggressive downward cast, continuing your power stroke almost to the water's surface before you stop the rod. Slicing down instead of out ensures that the energy of your cast slices through the wind rather than meeting the wind head-on. You can even make this downward motion more pronounced by reaching up with your arm

Wind can be tough on fly fishers, but there are usually solutions to wind problems, such as changing positions.

on the backcast and attempting to make the backcast on a more vertical angle so that the whole casting motion is more up-and-down than back-and-forth.

Another trick with a headwind, and with most winds in general, is to keep your casts low and off to your side. Because of friction produced when wind encounters the ground, the velocity of the wind is always a bit lower closer to the ground or water. And in all windy situations, it helps to shorten your leader and perhaps go to a heavier tippet size. Fish aren't as spooky when a breeze ruffles the water's surface, so you can often get away with a shorter, heavier leader. Don't try to make long hero casts in a big wind either. Try to get closer to the fish and make 30-foot casts, as few people can make an accurate cast at 60 feet with a strong wind blowing.

Of course, tailwinds aren't as bad but still require some adjustment, because a strong tailwind can push your backcast down too low or prevent it from straightening, and even with a tailwind, if you don't get a decent backcast, it's tough to make a nice forward cast. Put slightly more effort into your backcast by speeding up your stroke, then when you come forward, use just enough of a power stroke to get the line out in front of you. The tailwind should straighten it nicely, and it will settle to the water without much effort.

Side Winds

Assuming you are right-handed, a wind from left to right is not much of a problem as long as you compensate for the drift of your line as it settles to the water. A few practice casts will tell you how much you have to "lead" your target to the left to make it land where you want. As in dealing with headwinds and tailwinds, keeping the cast low and off to your side will minimize the effects of the wind.

A cross-body wind, or one from right to left if you are right-handed, is a serious issue. This wind blows the fly right into your body, and you must make some accommodation. One way is to turn your body 180 degrees, face where your backcast would have been, and then dump your backcast as your presentation cast. Another option when the wind is not as strong is to make a cross-body cast, which if you are a right-hander is a cast across your left shoulder instead of your right shoulder. Neither of these techniques are as fun or as accurate as making a standard overhead cast, but with a crosswind they are your only hope.

Of course, it goes without saying that when faced with a wind you should try to position your family so that they don't have to cast against either a headwind or a crosswind. Move to the other side of the river or to another shore if you are on a lake or pond. If you're in a boat, look for a place in the lee where the wind has been knocked down, or at least position the boat so that the caster does not have a crosswind or headwind. If fishing with a family all in the same boat or on the same piece of shoreline, it's always safest to limit the number of people fishing at one time in close quarters.

Fly Changes

So far I've downplayed the importance of having the right fly, and with the species of fish you'll be using to teach your family, fly selection is the least of your worries. But fly selection is also one of the fun puzzles we attempt to solve when fly fishing, and once you get beyond the more eager species, having the right fly can make a difference. Remember, though, it's not as if only one fly pattern in the world, Joe's Purple Upside-Down Grizzly Bugger, will be the only one that works, no matter what Joe tells you. It's just that sometimes the fly you use is too big,

Trying to figure out the right fly is one of the fun puzzles of fly fishing, but don't make it an agonizing situation.

or too small, or not the right shape. Fish hardly ever choose one color to the exclusion of all others, but you will find days when the color of your fly makes the difference between one fish and a half-dozen fish.

How do you know when to change flies? If you can't see fish, or if you don't know whether you are putting your fly over feeding fish, it's tough to tell. In a case like that, I'd pick a fly that was recommended by someone, or a fly that looks like the minnows or insects you see in the water—or maybe just a fly off in the corner of the fly box that speaks to you. And as long as I wasn't sure whether my fly was going over some fish, I'd try to cover as much water as possible and use that fly until I got sick of looking at it. However, if you see fish in the water or you see them feeding, you can make a more intelligent decision on changing flies.

Let's say you're fishing a clear stream for smallmouth bass, and you spot a few bass in the water. You cast a yellow popper over the bass and bring it back to you with a fairly vigorous retrieve. Occasionally a bass follows the fly, but turns away and never eats it. Before you switch flies, the first course of action should be to change your presentation. Cast the fly out and let it sit without motion for twenty seconds. Then give it a gentle twitch and let it sit again. Watch the reaction of the fish. If they show more interest and follow the fly for a longer distance, you're in the ballpark, and, of course, if you get a strike, you've solved the problem. If that doesn't work, try a really fast retrieve. But once you've tried a number of different presentations and you know the fish have seen the fly each time, it's time for a fly change.

In this case, since I was using a yellow popper, a bright surface fly, I would change to a dark subsurface fly like a black Woolly Bugger. And I'd go through the same variation on presentation until I was convinced my fly was of no interest. Then I might try a smaller fly, especially if one of the fish boiled at the fly but didn't connect.

The same philosophy holds true with trout, where you see fish feeding on a particular insect, except in this case you have a good clue as to what the fish might eat because you see some insects on the water. However, even with trout, the problem may be with your presentation and not the fly pattern, especially if you think drag is a problem. Sometimes drag on a fly is so subtle that you can't see it from 30 feet away, but a trout, inches away from the fly, sure can. It's always a good idea to change your position or try a slack-line cast on trout that won't eat your fly before you change flies.

Finding Fish in Streams

Whole books have been written about finding fish in streams; in fact, I've written a couple myself. But just turning your family loose in a stream without any guidance as to where fish might be living is a recipe for long faces. One of the best places to find fish in a stream is at the head of a pool,

Typical places to find trout in a river. Note that they prefer to be in slower water on the edge of fast water—especially along banks.

where fast riffled water dumps into slower, deeper water. That's where I'd put my family. Fish will always be found at the head of a pool, and these fish will often be the easiest to catch because the fast water hides mistakes in our presentation, and in the fast water fish have to make a quick decision. Don't rule out water at the head of a pool that looks too shallow. Fish will feed in pretty skinny water, so don't just have your family fish over the deepest water at the head of a pool.

In slower pools in a stream, look for trout adjacent to currents but just on the edge of the fastest current. Trout live in slower water and dart into the faster water, which offers more drifting food. Trout are not always in deep water and even big ones can feed in only a foot of water, as long as there is sufficient current to bring them food. However, if you're fishing for pike or smallmouth bass or carp in a stream, don't rule out backwaters and deeper, more stagnant places. Bass and pike are ambush feeders and often prowl the slower water in search of crayfish and minnows. And carp prefer slower currents, where they cruise in shallow water looking for their food.

Structure in a stream is always worth investigating, and not just rocks and logs in the middle of a river. Rocks, logs, and tiny projections in the bank of a river offer protection from predators and from the force of the current and also hold baitfish, so bass, pike, and trout will all be found near structure.

Finding Fish in Lakes

It's even harder to "read" a lake than a river or stream, because there is no current to define structure and places where fish live. In addition, while fish in moving water tend to stay put and let food come to them, in lakes they must cruise to find food. There is never a guarantee that fish will be in the water in front of you when you make your first cast.

Your first step should be to look for fish in shallow water. If you are fishing for sunfish, this is easy—they will invariably be found in the shallows, and if you are fishing during their spring spawning season, the light circular areas on the bottom where they've made nests will be far more visible than the fish themselves. Cast to these light spots even if you don't see a fish. Outside of the spawning season, look for sunfish and bass close to weed beds, lily pads, rocky points, and any place shallow water drops off into deeper water. Streams and rivers entering lakes are always hot spots because they wash food into the lake and also attract baitfish.

For fish that cruise open water, like white bass, striped bass, and trout, your first task should be to look carefully for signs of feeding fish. Trout make gentle rings on the surface when feeding on insects, but all of the open-water fish, when feeding on baitfish, make aggressive splashes and swirls that show up from hundreds of yards away. If you have a boat, it's perfectly all right to troll to find fish. Attach a nymph or small streamer to your line, let out 60 to 100 feet of line, and then slowly paddle or row the boat around the lake until you get a strike. Once you have located the fish this way, you can stop and cast for them. As always, don't leave the spinning rod at home. You can cover a lot more water with a spinning lure, and you may need the ability to search wide expanses of water with conventional tackle before you settle down and try to catch fish with a fly rod.

Finding Fish in Salt Water

Fishing in the ocean requires even more scouting and moving because, well, it's a big ocean and saltwater fish have the ability to move thousands of miles to find food. The one saving grace of fishing in salt water is that most of the species you fish for from shore or near shore are aggressive feeders, and if they are around, you will usually hook one. The problem is finding them. A school of striped bass that were all over a beach today may be 20 miles away tomorrow.

Your first line of attack should be to find places where people are already catching fish. Unlike fishing in lakes or wading trout streams, saltwater fly fishing has plenty of open space—usually. Don't crowd other anglers on jetties or crowded beaches, but if you see an angler hooked up on a rocky point or along a beach, it's perfectly acceptable to give him 100 yards of room and try for the same school of fish. Schools often move quickly, and the fish may be in front of you and your family in a matter of minutes. At least you know there are fish in the area, and probably also schools of baitfish that will attract other schools of gamefish.

Absent any other lucky anglers, look for points, offshore sandbars, weed lines, indentations in otherwise monotonous beaches where game-fish can corral prey, and especially places where bays or coastal rivers enter the ocean. Man-made structures like docks, jetties, and dredged channels will also attract gamefish. Use Google Earth to look for places where wide expanses of shallow water extend into deeper water. Shallow water means food: baitfish, crabs, shrimp, and squid. Although fish may prey on baitfish and squid over open water way offshore as well, the shal-lows are always teeming with critters saltwater gamefish like to eat.

While it pays to watch the tides for safety's sake, especially when wading in unfamiliar water, it's difficult to predict how the tides will affect fishing because in some areas an incoming tide is best, while in others an outgoing tide produces more fish, and in others a slack tide is best. Generally an incoming tide is best on shallow flats and sandbars and also on the insides of bays and estuaries. An outgoing tide is best for the outside edges of jetties and bays and the mouths of rivers.

An even better way to find concentrations of feeding fish is to fish at dawn and dusk. Regardless of the tide cycle, most of the saltwater game-fish we chase from shore will feed more actively at these times—and the start of an incoming tide at dawn or dusk will almost always produce some kind of gamefish activity!

Fly Rod Care

Fragile Tips

A fly rod that can land a 30-pound salmon without breaking a sweat can break in a millisecond when the angler doesn't pay attention. Tips on modern fly rods are strong when you flex them but very fragile in all other instances, and a broken rod is not a happy way to start a fishing expedition. Of course, you should pay attention around ceiling fans and screen doors, and a fly rod should never be put together inside because it's tough to get one outside without that fragile tip getting close to danger. It's also a good idea to avoid leaning a fly rod against a car because the wind can blow it over where it can get stepped on or smashed when someone closes the door. Lean a fly rod against a tree or bush with the tip up in the air, and alert all members of the family to where you've just placed your rod.

Walking to the river, especially if you have to negotiate trees and brush, is another danger zone. It's a good idea to wait until you get to the river to string up the rods, and they should be carried in their rod tubes or at least in their cloth sacks because it's easy to drop a piece of a rod on the way to the river without realizing it. I've noticed that kids are especially dangerous when walking with strung-up rods, as for some reason they always point the tip of the rod toward the ground. Rods should always be carried with the tip upright when walking from one spot to another.

Stringing up rods is another time when they often break. Don't try to yank the fly line out of a rod by pulling down on the leader. Fly rods are not designed to flex at an acute angle. Lay the rod on the ground or have another member of your family hold it, and then pull at least 10 feet of fly line outside of the tip of the rod before you begin fishing.

Getting Stuck in Trees

Impress on your family that they *will* get their flies stuck in trees on their first trip and then on every fly-fishing trip they take for the rest of their lives. In fact, if you're the teacher, I suggest you make sure that your first cast ends up in the trees, laugh about it, and then carefully retrieve the fly, setting a good example.

The best way to retrieve a fly from a tree is to first attempt to jiggle it loose. Point the tip of the rod directly at the fly, gently tighten the line until all the slack is out of it, and then wiggle the rod tip gently from side to side. Often this will dislodge a fly on the first attempt. Yanking on a fly as soon as it lands in a tree will often drive the hook deep into a branch, or if enough force is used, the leader will wrap itself around the branch. Additionally, trying to yank a fly out of a tree can break a rod. Abrupt pulls on the rod may wrap the line around the tip of the rod, and the next tug can snap the tip like a twig.

If the wiggle method doesn't work and the fly is within reach, lay the rod down carefully on the ground where it won't get stepped on, follow the line to the fly, and remove the fly. Don't carry the rod with you to the tree—this often results in further tangles along the way. If the fly is too high to remove by hand, you may have to risk losing it. Point the rod tip directly at the fly and either strip line or walk slowly backward until the fly comes loose or it breaks off. It's important to face away from the fly when doing this, as the fly can suddenly come loose and snap back into your face.

Of course, you can avoid fly losses by trying to find a place to fish without nearby trees, but that isn't always possible since fish tend to hang near cover. But pay attention to the area behind all members of your family before you turn them loose. You might be able to find a place with more clearance behind them. One additional suggestion is to keep casts short. Twenty-foot casts are much less likely to get out of control, and for novices short, accurate casts are far better than trying to handle 50 feet of line in the air.

Flies may also get caught in the rocks or low grasses behind your family, even when there are no trees in sight. When this happens, remind them to keep their backcasts higher by making an abrupt stop with the rod tip just past the vertical.

Nymphs and streamers stuck on the bottom should be removed in a similar way. Try to move to the same side of the submerged rock or log where you think the fly got stuck (usually the upstream side in a river), and gently wiggle the tip. If that fails, again walk backward with the tip of the rod pointed directly at the fly, keeping your face turned away from it.

You will lose flies in a day of fishing. They're expendable. Even seasoned fly fishers will lose a half-dozen flies or more in a day. Make sure you don't show any disappointment when a member of your family loses a fly, and don't throw a fit when you snap one off.

Chapter 8

The Family Fly-Fishing Vacation

If your family learns to enjoy fly fishing together, eventually you'll want to plan a real family fishing vacation. It might be a weekend trip or it might turn out to be several weeks in duration. Especially with kids, one of the best ways to encourage their enthusiasm is to make fly fishing part of a bigger adventure, whether it is a camping trip to a state or national park, a canoe trip to remote northern lakes, a horseback excursion to a high mountain lake, or a week at a ranch or lodge that specializes in fishing.

The most important point to remember is that not all members of your family will have the same expectations or desires when it comes to the fishing part of the trip. If the long-anticipated vacation turns out to be mostly fishing with little else of interest, you'll have a lot harder time convincing your family to take a fishing vacation when the next opportunity presents itself.

Jim Hickey, an experienced guide from Wyoming, has seen many variations on the family fly-fishing vacation and has found that when the family groups are small (one or two parents and one child), the trips are more likely to be a success than when six family members all try to enjoy the same experience at once. He related one family trip that was extremely successful for the parents and their two kids, but they had to divide and conquer to make it work. "One guide took the two parents in his boat and they fished all day," he told me, "while the other guide took the two kids. The kids fished safely a little bit with the guide, but then they swam, caught frogs, and collected rocks and ate a great lunch." At the end of the day, everybody had a great time and no one was bored—the kids stayed active and the parents got to fish all day without interruption.

Camping and Hiking Trips

Hiking and/or camping trips are one way to turn a fly-fishing trip into an adventure. It's also a way to ensure that fly fishing does not overwhelm the vacation and become its sole purpose, as the fishing necessarily becomes a sideshow and not the main event. Fly fishing becomes a natural part of the adventure because your family is already outdoors, and fishing may actually provide some of the meals for the trip. The space and weight limitations of camping and hiking trips also play well into the philosophy of family fly-fishing trips, because the gear needs to be simple and stripped down.

Hiking to a remote pond or stream, or getting there on horseback or by canoe, makes the destination a lot more special than driving the car to a roadside parking spot. The anticipation as you and your family approach that alpine lake or remote wilderness stream builds suspense, and even if the fishing is poor, you've still enjoyed a great adventure together. In addition, fishing spots away from civilization usually offer easier fishing because the fish don't see as many anglers. Remote locations are also often less fertile than fishing spots lower in the valleys where we locate most of our civilization. Infertile waters hold fish that don't agonize over what they eat, and fly selection is often a matter of just getting a fly in front of the fish. Remote locations in the East are more likely to support brook trout, which are about the easiest trout to catch on a fly, and remote areas in the West are most likely to offer either native cutthroat trout, an equally gullible fish, or introduced eastern brook trout.

Keep fly-fishing gear for hiking and backpacking simple. An 8- to 9-foot fly rod for a 5- or 6-weight fly line paired with a floating line is all you will usually need for trout fishing in remote lakes and ponds. Most rods today are made in four-piece versions, which can be easily strapped to the side of a backpack frame, stowed in a canoe, or strapped to a saddle. Some rods are available in five- or six-piece versions, which pack down even shorter. Bring a few 9-foot leaders, some tippet material, and a box of flies that includes a half-dozen dry flies, nymphs, and streamers recommended for the area. Leave the waders and fishing vest at home.

Hiking and camping are ways to combine fly fishing with other family-oriented outdoor activities. COURTESY JON LUKE

They're heavy and hard to pack, and you can fish from shore or wade with shorts and sneakers or hiking boots. You can carry all the flies you need in a pocket.

Camping from a car or RV is also a smart way to ease into the family fly-fishing vacation. Pick a campground on a river or lake, and do some research prior to the trip to make sure the body of water where you are camping has good fishing within walking or boating distance. If you're on a lake, see if boat rentals are available; if not, plan on bringing your own canoe or kayaks or float tubes. Casting from shore might be difficult if you can't wade out very far and the shoreline is covered with trees. You may not be able to find a camping spot with world-class trout fishing right outside of your tent, but you may find stocked trout or bass and panfish. Being right on the water means that those in the family who want to go fishing have access anytime they want, and those who don't want to fish or only want to fish for an hour at a time can return to camp for other activities. It's one of the best ways to alleviate the problems of differing wishes and expectations among family members.

Camping and fishing on a canoe trip might bring you into habitat more suitable for bass, pike, and panfish. This is particularly true in the upper Midwest and in lower-altitude lakes in the Northeast, where water temperatures are too warm to support trout. In that case, a 9-foot rod for a 7- or 8-weight line along with a matching reel with a floating line and some 12- and 16-pound leaders will be all the gear you need, besides snips and a pair of pliers or forceps to remove hooks. Flies here can be very simple—a few poppers in various sizes and colors and a few subsurface streamers for fishing slightly deeper water.

Guided Boat Trips

One way to have a family vacation with fly fishing is to hire a guide for just a day or two within the confines of a larger trip. It could be a trip to the Rocky Mountains, where the family spends a day floating in a drift boat with a trout-fishing guide, or a side trip for saltwater fishing during a trip to Florida, the Bahamas, or Belize. Bear in mind that even numbers

Fly fishing together in a drift boat with a guide can be a great activity for couples.

are always better than odd numbers for trips like this, because most of these trips involve boats that are designed to accommodate two anglers and a guide. If you have an odd number in your family, either someone will have to sit out or you'll need to hire a second boat. Most saltwater flats boats can accommodate a child and two adults without creating a problem, but the drift boats used on rivers only handle two people safely.

And always inform your guide beforehand if you're bringing a child along. A guide that expects only adults on a trip may not have the room to comfortably handle two adults and a child, but even more critically, he might not have the proper-size personal flotation device for a child, which could put your child in serious danger. Besides, some guides are just not great with kids. Before booking a trip involving children, feel the guide out first. If he or she immediately sounds enthusiastic and says something like, "I love having kids along—I take them all the time," you've probably got a good fit. If the mention of children elicits a long pause, or if the guide balks in the slightest at having kids along on a trip, your best course of action is to find another guide.

If your family group involves three or more people, you'll have to consider multiple boats and multiple guides. Before you even leave home, you should decide who is going to fish with whom. Will kids fish together with a guide and both parents fish together, or will one parent fish with one child and one with the other? Or perhaps you'll start out one way, then arrange with both guides to meet at lunch and switch partners, or perhaps for the last half of the day both kids will be in the same boat. It's likely they will be tired of fishing and want to stop and collect rocks on gravel bars or chase minnows in the shallows for the rest of the day. Again, let the guides know what you plan on doing well in advance. One guide may be better with kids than the other, and you'll have to trust them to work out the logistics before your trip.

Boat Considerations

In the typical trout-fishing trip from a raft or drift boat, both anglers can fish simultaneously if a few simple rules are followed. First, know your directions. Using the numbers on a clock as a reference, which all guides do when giving directions, remember that 12 o'clock is directly off the bow, 6 o'clock is directly behind the boat, 3 o'clock is on the right side when facing the bow, and 9 o'clock is on the left. These numbers don't change no matter which direction you're looking—they are always in relation to the boat.

Never cast at 12 o'clock or 6 o'clock. Both of these angles put your cast directly over your partner and the guide, and hooking a guide is not a good way to begin your day. The person in the bow should concentrate on fishing on the left side of the boat if he or she is right-handed, or the right side of the boat if left-handed. The person in the stern, behind the guide, casts in the opposite direction. Accomplished casters can cast with the rod tip over the shoulder opposite of their normal casting side or roll cast if both anglers want to concentrate on the same side of the boat, but if you can't cast easily and safely in one direction, just sit tight for a few minutes. The boat will soon be in different water where you may have a better shot.

The angler in the stern is also responsible for ensuring that casts don't get tangled. The person in the bow can't be expected to turn around to see when the angler in the stern is casting, so the responsibility falls to the stern angler. Because the bow is most often the best position for fishing (this angler gets first crack at new water), it pays to switch positions throughout the day.

Most guides also like to use the oars, which are almost always sticking out at 90 degrees to the boat. They are the dividing line between bow and stern angler. If the person in the bow fishes any farther back than the oars, the person in the stern runs out of water to fish without crossing over the other angler's line—plus the angler in the bow will likely get his or her fly caught in the oars. For the same reason, the angler in the stern should stay slightly behind the oars.

In saltwater flats boats, the guide runs the motor and also poles the boat through shallow water from the stern, and because flats boats are pretty tight, it's rare for both fly fishers to cast at the same time. This is important to understand when both of you are fanatic anglers—you'll only get half as much fishing in a flats boat as you would when wading the flats or trout fishing from a drift boat. So if you're planning a saltwater fly-fishing trip with your spouse, take along a camera if you need to keep busy, or plan on sitting back and enjoying the scenery for half the day. One other alternative might be to take a spinning rod, as it is often possible for one angler to fly fish off the bow of a flats boat while the other casts a spin rod from the center.

Guided Walk/Wade Trips

Although most guided trout-fishing trips these days are done from drift boats, with three people you might consider a walk/wade trip, which is exactly what it sounds like. You drive with a guide to a river and then hike along the banks and fish the better water on foot. With three people the guide can stay in sight and work back and forth between anglers so that everyone gets the benefit of his or her attention, but the more self-sufficient anglers can mostly fend for themselves. If this

A walk/wade trip with a guide allows you a little more flexibility and the opportunity to spend more time in one place.

sounds appealing, make sure you arrange it in advance. Not all guides offer walk/wade trips, and not all of them like to fish this way.

Before you embark on a walk/wade trip, make sure you understand the logistics of the trip. How far from a vehicle will you be in the middle of the day? How much will you have to carry? Usually the guide carries lunch and most of the gear, but the guide should understand the physical limitations of your family before the trip. You don't want to drag a seven-year-old on a 3-mile hike in waders, nor do you want a young child wading a fast river without constant supervision. In fact, you probably don't want small children wading fast, deep rivers at all, but there is always a chance the guide knows some smaller streams more appropriate to the size of your child.

Guides in salt water are less likely to offer walk/wade trips because not all locations offer good fishing from the beach, but in some places, notably the striped bass fisheries in the Northeast and, to a lesser extent, the sea trout and redfish flats from South Carolina through the Gulf of Mexico, you may find a "land captain" specializing in wading trips. However, it's unlikely that you'll find a saltwater guide in Mexico, Belize, or the Bahamas willing to do a wade-only trip without the use of a boat.

Fishing Lodges and Ranches

Fishing lodges and ranches run the gamut from pampered and elegant to rustic and basic, from locations that offer world-class dining by trained chefs and rooms or cabins right out of *Town & Country* to plain rooms with "home-cooked meals." Prices vary accordingly, from just over $1,000 a week for drive-to Canadian lodges to over $10,000 per week for a high-end lodge in Colorado on private trout water.

Regardless of what type of lodge you choose, it's a large investment in a vacation for a family, and it pays to do exhaustive research before you pick a location. First you should decide what kind of fishing you'd like for your family. Do you want to chase wilderness trout, large northern pike, Atlantic salmon, steelhead, saltwater species, or bass and panfish? Pike and bass lodges are less expensive, saltwater locations are typically

Some lodges, such as Rawah Ranch in Colorado, are very family friendly while others are not. It's always best to do a thorough check before taking the whole family to a fishing lodge.

at the pricey end, and Atlantic salmon trips are very expensive, with a good chance of catching few or no fish depending on water conditions. Trout lodges run the gamut. Some lodges offer a mixed bag of species, but they usually concentrate on just one or two fish. A good way to check is to look at the species shown in the lodge's photo gallery to see what kind of fish the guests regularly catch. For instance, many Canadian pike and bass lodges have excellent trout fishing in the area, but the owners and guides may not be familiar with the trout waters or the habits of the local trout through the season. Their bread and butter might be guiding anglers in search of pike and bass, and thus trout may be available but there may be no one to show you how or where to catch them.

If you just want to catch fish easily, pick a bass or pike trip, or lay out a large amount of cash for an Alaskan lodge, where trout, salmon, pike, and grayling are almost guaranteed. Trout fishing, salmon fishing, and saltwater fly fishing are more fickle and very weather-dependent. A week of 20 mph winds can turn a bonefishing trip into an extended board game tournament; hot, clear weather will make an Atlantic salmon trip a casting (not catching) exercise; and torrential rains often turn trout rivers into unfishable chocolate milk. You can hedge your bets by staying away from the shoulder seasons with reduced rates offered by some lodges. These trips are for experienced anglers who understand the risk. Your family may not be as understanding.

One way to at least find out that a lodge is truthful in its claims and that the rooms are clean, the food is edible, and the boats and other vehicles are in good working order is to book through a travel agency specializing in fly fishing, or stick to lodges that are endorsed by a fly-fishing company with a reputation to uphold. For instance, Orvis has strict rules on rooms, food, transportation, safety, and fly-fishing knowledge in its Endorsed Lodge program (www.orvis.com/endorsed). This does not mean that all the lodges in the program are homogeneous—far from it— but rather that each lodge has been inspected and vetted with an eye on ensuring that customers have an experience that lives up to their expectations. Even so, some lodges are family-oriented and others are not. But when you book through a lodge that is certified by a reliable company, you can at least ensure that the owner or manager will be honest with you when you ask about necessities for your entire family.

Trout Lodges

Make sure that the lodge or ranch you choose specializes in fly fishing. "Oh, yeah, we fly fish too" is not an acceptable answer unless your entire family is experienced in fly fishing and all are capable of finding fish, choosing flies, and tying knots by themselves. Study a prospective lodge's website with a fine-tooth comb. Make calls and talk to the lodge managers (not their marketing people!) to make sure they understand you are bringing your family and everyone wants to fly fish at least part of the time. If you have any rank novices in your family, let them know. Most professional fly-fishing guides are excellent teachers, but you want to make sure that a good teacher will be on hand the week you take your trip before you even think of making a deposit.

Make sure you discuss your expectations with the lodge manager prior to booking. Many trout-fishing lodges concentrate on float fishing because it's a great way to cover a long stretch of river, catch a lot of trout, and see a variety of scenery. But many couples and families prefer to wade smaller streams or may want to enjoy a mixture of wading and floating. Some lodges offer only fishing on lakes and ponds. If you and your family have your hearts set on fishing rivers and streams, you could be in for a big disappointment. In addition, some lodges are located on a single river and have no other options within driving distance. It's probably a very good river if that's the case, but decide if you really want to see the same type of water every day or if you want a more varied experience, even if it means you'll catch smaller and fewer fish.

The best lodges for family fly fishing offer a combination of float fishing on larger rivers for the more experienced, wade fishing on small streams for the intermediate-level angler, and stocked pond fishing on the property for the novices. Another addition, which makes a great family adventure, is a pack trip into a high mountain lake. With horses or llamas to carry food and float tubes, the family can hike or ride into a pristine lake above timberline without having to carry a thirty-pound pack, and the float tubes enable everyone to get out into the best fishing in the lake.

If you're sure not everyone in the family wants to fish every day, or if some in your family only want to fish half days, make sure you have these options. Float trips are typically all-day events because the boats are dropped off at one location and the trailers are then moved by a shuttle service to the take-out point, which the guide may plan on reaching any time from late afternoon to dark. Some locations offer short floats or half-day floats, so if someone in your family would prefer a half-day float, make sure shorter floats are offered. In some rivers, put-in and take-out locations are extremely limited and short floats just might not be possible.

It's unlikely that everyone in your family will want to fish all day, every day. Be very careful about ensuring that other activities are available at a ranch or lodge on a regular and consistent basis. Some lodges are strictly fishing lodges and are located in places that don't offer any activities for non-fishing family members or those who might not want to fish every day—unless they are perfectly content to sit on the porch of a lodge and read. I can think of a couple of great fishing lodges, located on world-class trout streams, that offer virtually nothing for the non-fishing guest. The towns in the area consist of a bar and a general store, and the surrounding countryside is hot, dry high desert that doesn't even offer the possibility of an interesting hike.

Other lodges offer activities that are described in their brochures or on their website, but without sufficient variety, they might not interest your family for more than a few hours, and the supposed activities might only be available if Susie the assistant chef has the day off and can borrow someone's car. If the lodge or ranch offers kayaking or bird watching or horseback riding, make sure they have a full-time kayak guide or naturalist or wrangler on the payroll. Be careful of wording like this, taken from an actual lodge website: "The staff can help arrange fishing, horseback riding, and personalized area tours from the resort for your convenience. They will also arrange historical and archeological tours in the area." Yeah, the staff might be able to arrange these trips or they might not. They probably have no control over the quality of the experience, and for sure you will have to pay extra for these activities, things that you could have arranged on your own while staying in a motel.

Many lodges offer pick-up service from the local airport, driving you directly to their location. This is a nice convenience, but if you're on a family trip and you suspect someone may want to stray off the ranch to partake in other activities, or if you're not absolutely sure the lodge offers these activities as part of their package (and if you want to ensure that you don't get taken on a tour of Yellowstone Park with a family of screaming kids or obnoxious parents), it might be worth the extra money to rent a car to make sure you are not all stranded at the lodge for a week.

It may be self-evident, but I should also mention that children are not welcome at all fishing lodges. Some don't allow kids at all, some take them reluctantly, and many just don't have much for younger children to do. If you have young children along on your trip who might only be capable of fishing for an hour on the ranch pond, check to see if the lodge offers day-care service and special activities for younger children. Make sure they spell it out, like this ranch in Montana does: "Children are a focus of activities and recreation here at the Lodge. [The lodge] has a unique children's program where family interaction is key and children have the freedom to roam the property and the various activities as they'd like. Children focused activities include daily kids rides, daily arts and crafts, water activities, kids teepee overnight, kids rodeo, organized games and a junior wrangler program to name a few. Your child will fall in love with [our lodge] and make friendships that can last a lifetime." With that kind of wording, I'd take my seven-year-old to that lodge in a heartbeat—as long as I did my homework to make sure the fishing is interesting!

Saltwater Lodges

Saltwater fishing lodges are typically located in tropical and subtropical locations, which make them the perfect getaway for northerners craving warmth and sunshine during the winter. However, many of these locations also offer terrific fly fishing during the spring, summer, and fall months, as it is often no hotter in the Bahamas or Belize or Mexico in July than it is in Atlanta or New York. Tropical species like bonefish, permit, and tarpon feed year-round, and as long as a hurricane doesn't threaten, winds are often lighter during the summer than in the winter, making casting much easier. Sometimes the water gets too hot in summer in the middle of the day for good fishing, but that works out perfectly for a family vacation because fishing is done in the evening and early morning, allowing the family to enjoy other activities during the day.

Most saltwater lodges offer snorkeling or scuba diving as an activity for the non-fishing members of the family, and most have kayaks or small sailboats that can be used by guests. These trips are great for young children because the shallows located near saltwater lodges are often calm, warm, and full of aquatic life that can fascinate a five-year-old for hours.

As in any kind of planning involving fishing lodges, it's critical to do your homework first. Make sure the lodge specializes in fly fishing, and let them know how many anglers and how many non-anglers you'll be bringing, and their abilities. Unlike most trout-fishing lodges, it's

Saltwater fishing lodges are very appealing in the middle of winter, as much for lying on the beach as for great fishing. This view of the dock at El Pescador Lodge in Belize, a lodge that is very family friendly, shows that it's not all about fishing.

unlikely that you'll be able to purchase additional flies, leaders, tippet, or fly lines at the lodge, and saltwater guides in many tropical locations rarely bring along flies, rods, reels, or extra leaders. This is not the case with all lodges, but a lodge that offers even a supply of local fly patterns for sale is the exception rather than the rule. It's best to research the fishery first to find out what kind of tackle you'll need, or book your trip through an outfit that specializes in fly-fishing vacations, as these operations publish detailed pre-trip information that contains checklists for everything you'll need.

Most novice fly casters can manage to hack through a trout- or bass-fishing trip with a fly rod and still catch some fish, but this is typically not the case with saltwater trips. The main difference is that with trout fishing, the fish stay put and you can get closer to them or move into an easier position by wading or by manipulating the boat. In saltwater fly fishing the fish always move, sometimes quickly, and it's essential to be able to place the fly accurately with a minimum of false casting. This does not mean everyone in your family should be able to cast 60 feet. Most bonefish, tarpon, and permit are caught between 20 and 40 feet away. However, quick accurate casts and the ability to deal with wind are essential. Everyone in the family should practice casting or take a brush-up lesson from a casting instructor before the trip.

I have seen too many decent trout anglers come away from a saltwater fly-fishing trip in frustration because they had not bothered to practice casting before the trip and could not deliver the fly properly. The basics of proper fly casting in salt water are not different from the basics of any other type of fly fishing, but unlike in trout fishing, where you can still catch fish with a sloppy cast, saltwater fly fishing requires better timing, which helps straighten the leader and drive the fly into the wind.

I'd also recommend that all members of your family learn to double haul before a saltwater trip. The double haul is a technique that increases line speed and helps with both distance and dealing with wind. It's not often needed in trout fishing, but saltwater fishing without the ability to double haul can lead to frustration. An advanced casting lesson or some practice after looking at a casting book or video will help your family learn this technique, but it takes a while to develop the muscle memory to execute the double haul. Don't plan on having them learn it once they get to the lodge. You don't want to spend your valuable vacation time doing casting drills.

DIY Trips

Perhaps you can't afford a fishing lodge or guide, or would prefer to plan a trip with your family that has more flexibility. DIY, or do-it-yourself, trips can be economical, and many people take great pleasure in discovering new locations and new techniques on their own. This approach can lend a sense of adventure to a fly-fishing trip when it goes mostly right, but with poor planning and bad luck, your family may find themselves in the middle of a Chevy Chase movie. When you book with an experienced guide or lodge, they'll do most of the planning for you—they'll know where the fishing is best, they'll tailor the degree of difficulty to your family's abilities, and they'll make sure a lunch is packed. A good guide will fix leaders, change flies, and offer casting advice for everyone in your family. On a DIY trip all that becomes your responsibility.

On a DIY trip you'll probably be staying in motels or camping in an RV or in a tent. You'll have everything you need in an RV, but if you plan on playing the nomad from motel to motel, you'll have to make sure you have a cooler for lunches and drinks, and you'll have to plan each day's lunch the night before. You'll need to pay attention to weather reports because if it rains 2 inches overnight, your strategy of fishing a big river should be shelved and replaced by a trip to a small stream or a lake, where severe runoff won't affect the fishing as much.

But the big planning should happen long before you bunk down in a motel for the first night. Your route should include locations with lots of options for public fishing and just as many options for non-fishing activities. Be very careful about access. Perhaps you read an article in a magazine about a great river in Colorado that sounds like a scenic place with relatively easy fishing for the whole family. You fly to Denver, rent a car, and book a couple of rooms in a motel near the river, and the next morning you drive to the river, only to discover that it has absolutely no public access. Colorado is particularly dicey because if a private landowner owns both banks, he can keep you out of the river entirely, and Colorado also does not require landowners to mark private property as such. If you are unfamiliar with an area, sometimes the only way you find out whether a stretch of river is private or public is when you are asked to leave or are arrested for trespassing. This is not a good way to begin a family fly-fishing trip.

Wyoming, Utah, Virginia, and Colorado are among the states that have the most restrictive river-access laws. Montana, Pennsylvania, Michigan, and Vermont are among the states that allow fishing and wading in a river up to the high-water line, as long as you access the water at a public place like a highway bridge or public fishing access site, and then stay within the high-water line when walking along the banks.

NOTICE

**SPECIAL TROUT FISHING
REGULATIONS APPLY:**

- ALL TROUT CAUGHT SHALL BE
  IMMEDIATELY RETURNED TO THE
  WATER WITHOUT UNNECESSARY INJURY.
- ONLY ARTIFICIAL LURES ARE PERMITTED.
- USE OF NATURAL BAIT, DEAD OR ALIVE,
  FOR ANY SPECIES, PROHIBITED.

SEASON: ALL YEAR

N.Y.S. DEPT. OF ENVIRONMENTAL CONSERVATION, ALBANY,N.Y. 12233

**ARTIFICIAL
LURES
ONLY**

N.Y.S. DEPT. OF ENVIRONMENTAL CONSERVATION, ALBANY, N.Y. 12233

Some states mark their public fishing areas and special regulations sections very well. Other states are not so diligent.

Every state has different laws and different interpretations of access laws, so before you plan any kind of DIY trip, always research both public access areas and access laws along your route so that you can ensure that your family can fish that river you've always wanted to show them.

You can avoid such issues by taking your trip to Montana or Pennsylvania or Vermont, or by planning your trip within national parks or national forests, places where *you* own the water and the land. National parks in particular offer some wonderful fishing, and contrary to what you might think, it's often of excellent quality and not overfished. For instance, Yellowstone National Park has a number of major trout rivers within its boundaries, including the headwaters of the Madison, Gallatin, and Yellowstone Rivers, as well as the Lamar River, the Firehole River, Slough Creek, Lewis Creek, and the Gibbon River, plus many smaller, remote creeks and lakes. The great thing about Yellowstone is that floating the rivers in drift boats is not allowed within the park, which cuts down the fishing traffic by a large margin because most anglers don't like to hike very far. Even in the middle of the tourist season, you can often enjoy long stretches of river where you might see more bison or elk than other anglers.

Chapter 9

Fly Fishing Safely

Fly fishing is not a risky sport, but people die every year on fly-fishing trips, usually from drowning. When you take trips alone, safety is probably not something you dwell on, but with the precious cargo of your family along, some of the things you did for excitement on solo trips become cause for concern.

Wading Safety

Drowning by careless wading is one of the main causes of death and injury when fly fishing. Your first order of business should be to ensure that all members of your family are adequate swimmers. Getting out of a dangerous situation doesn't require someone to be a strong swimmer—they usually just need to keep their head above water and dog-paddle to a shallow spot. But the more comfortable someone is when submerged in water, the less likely they are to panic and make a bad situation treacherous.

Choose Water Accordingly

The water you fish with your family should be chosen based on their abilities. If everyone in your family is a strong swimmer and they know how to wade fast water, walking into a remote canyon with big boulders and tumbling rapids can be an exhilarating experience. But if you have young children, pick a river or a stretch of river with gentle shallows, a gravel or sand bottom, and a slow to moderate current. The larger the rocks in the streambed, the more dangerous the wading will be. You can

Always cross at shallow riffles or tails of pools, and if the water is rough even there, use the buddy system. COURTESY JON LUKE

slip off the edges of the rocks, and even large flat rocks can cause problems. They may be slick, and while they might look flat from above, a tiny slope combined with current can push even a strong adult into a deep hole as if sliding on an icy hill.

Always inspect the water well upstream or downstream of where you intend to fish. If one of your kids wanders off to explore by herself, you want to make sure she can't find herself in a dangerous situation. Don't forget that not only do most kids think they're invincible, but because they are shorter than us, they also can't see deep holes as well from their lower vantage point. If you can't see bottom, chances are the water is dangerous. Try to pick a stretch of a big river without deep holes, or pick smaller streams without large, deep pools. Trout and bass only need a foot or so of water to feed, so don't assume that just because there are no deep holes in sight, the fishing will not be productive.

Know Where and How to Cross

Fishing only from one side of a river often leaves you in less desirable fishing spots. There may be streamside brush or less attractive riffles or fish feeding just out of reach. Eventually you and your family will want to cross a river. First, I suggest that you all cross together—if someone falls in, the whole family will be there to help. In addition, smaller kids can be helped across fast water by having one adult or larger child on either side of them, or sometimes only one larger person. The stronger wader should always be on the downstream side of the smaller child so he can brace himself as he walks. Holding hands tightly or locking arms makes this process safe and easy as long as the adults don't have any problem as well. Before taking any small child across a piece of fast water, one adult should cross first to make sure there are no unseen drop-offs along the way.

Tails of pools and wide riffles are usually the best places to cross. Riffles in particular are safer to cross because the turbulence in the water reduces its downstream velocity, but that has to be balanced with visibility. It's harder to see bottom in a riffle and easier to see obstructions in the smooth tail of a pool, so choose carefully. Also look for expansive patches

Safe wading techniques include keeping your body sideways to the current, using a wading staff, crossing at an upstream angle, and feeling your way carefully along the bottom.

of sand or gravel instead of large rocks. Large rocks are often slippery and feet can get wedged between them, throwing the wader off balance. Also be aware that rocks in shallow water may be slipperier than rocks in fast current—in the more placid shallows, algae builds up on rocks, making them slick as greased soccer balls. Don't let your guard down even if you've already gotten through the fast, deep current. Falling in shallow water can potentially be even more dangerous because of the possibility of a broken bone.

Wading Technique

Wading through difficult water is more like shuffling than walking. Make sure you give everyone in your family a short lesson in wading safety before they try any wading. Here are some important tips to share with your family:

- Never step where you can't see. If the water is too dirty for you to see bottom, even in the shallows, restrict your wading to gravel bars with sloping shores.

- Shuffle your feet along the bottom, making sure that your lead foot has a secure purchase before bringing the other foot forward.

- Never step on top of a rock when you can shuffle around it. Rocks are often slippery.

- Be careful when sliding around a big rock that your foot does not get wedged between the large rock and a smaller one below it.

- Look for light patches on the bottom. They usually indicate patches of sand and gravel, which are much easier to negotiate than a rocky bottom.

- Never cross your legs when wading. This is a sure way to lose your balance.

- Try to keep your body weight immediately above your feet. Don't make long reaches with one foot.

- Cross a river at an upstream angle. This way, if the current gets too strong or if you wade into water that is too deep, you can retrace your steps. If you wade at a downstream angle, you may get pushed into a hole and be unable to get back upstream.

- If you have to turn your body, always do it in an upstream direction. Turning downstream against a strong current can make you walk into a deep hole whether you want to or not, because you will keep walking instinctively to maintain your balance.

- Try to keep the wide part of your body at right angles to the current. This will give you a smaller profile against the force of the current and less water resistance.

Dress for Success

It's hard to find waders to fit kids, but that may be a good thing. If the water is cold, consider hip boots. They are sometimes easier to find and they help keep kids in shallower water—plus it's easier to swim in hip boots than in waders. Kids and smaller adults should never wade above their knees when starting out. A lot of wading technique is just developing confidence and experience. By sticking to the shallows at first, they'll learn how to walk on slippery and uneven bottoms before they have to face strong currents.

A much better option for inexperienced waders during the summer is to wade "wet," which means using good wading shoes with either short pants or quick-drying long pants. It's much easier to swim if they fall in, and the treacherous situation of having a pair of waders that act like a sea anchor, pulling them downstream against their will, is eliminated. It will also be easier for them to climb over rocks and logs without the restriction that waders sometimes offer. If the water and air are warm enough, it's just plain more fun to leave those big rubber pants behind.

Regardless of whether your family wears waders or not, good wading shoes are not optional, unless you wade only in shallow areas with fine gravel and sand, in which case old sneakers or water sandals will work. But once you get into any situation with larger rocks, sturdy wading shoes with either felt soles or rubber soles with metal studs are essential. Wading shoes offer better ankle support for more stability, and the thicker wading shoes protect against stone bruises. I'll discuss the environmental implications of felt and rubber soles in the next chapter, but for safety, felt soles with or without metal studs are very secure on slippery bottoms. In my experience, wading shoes with rubber soles must also contain carbide studs for security. I've tested all kinds of products for wading on slippery rocks, and despite the claims of many manufacturers, even "sticky rubber" soles do not offer enough insurance against slipping unless they are accompanied by some kind of metal studs, and carbide studs are the best.

When wearing chest-high or waist-high waders, the most important piece of gear is also the cheapest—a secure wading belt. These are simply nylon belts with a strong locking mechanism and a quick-release

Nylon wading belts with a quick-release feature are inexpensive and easy to use. Most waders come with one. Make sure everyone in your family wears a wading belt, as this simple item could save the life of a loved one.
COURTESY ORVIS

buckle. They should be secured tightly around the waist, tight enough so that you can't reach into your pants pockets when the belt is attached. The reason for a wading belt is to keep air inside the lower part of the waders if you take a spill, which not only keeps you dry in a quick dunk, but also prevents your waders from filling with water if you get sucked into a deep hole. The air trapped inside the wader legs gives you some buoyancy and prevents the waders from acting as a sea anchor. Without a belt, if your body faces downstream and water rushes into the waders right down to your legs, you may be unable to maneuver enough to get to shallow water safely and can get sucked into a strong hydraulic with no hope of getting out. And when you do finally reach shallow water, waders completely filled with water are so heavy that some people can't even stand upright.

With kids or weak swimmers, it's even a good idea to have them wear two wading belts—one tightly around the waist and the other right at the top of the waders. This is even further security against water getting inside the waders. Wader belts should not be made of very stretchy material (as they were in the past), because those don't keep water out under the pressure of the current. Stiffer nylon webbing is best, and the belt should always have a secure quick-release mechanism. If you get hung up on a snag because of your wading belt, you must be able to remove it quickly.

If you are fishing with kids, make sure you get them a wading belt that offers continuous adjustments, not the kind that gets to a certain point and will not adjust any tighter. Wader belts are designed with adults in mind, and the fancy ones with multiple adjustments may not get tight enough to fit around an eight-year-old's tiny waist. The simplest wading belts, consisting of a long piece of nylon that slips into a locking mechanism, can be adjusted down to the smallest size, after which you can just cut off the excess nylon so it does not get in the way.

If you fall into the water with waders on, you will not tip upside down with your legs in the air. I'm not sure why this myth is still perpetuated, as the great fly fisherman Lee Wulff disproved this silly notion back in the 1930s by jumping off a bridge with his waders on. No matter how hard he tried, he could not keep his legs in the air with his head submerged.

Get Wading Staffs for the Whole Family

Wading staffs used to be the exclusive province of old, frail guys, but you now find all smart anglers using them. When you have the entire family in a river at the same time, it's a good idea for everyone to have one. A wading staff becomes a third point of balance, and in fast, slippery water it's amazing how much additional confidence and security a staff can offer. Staffs can be used to probe ahead for deep spots and big rocks, and used on your downstream side, they can give you balance when crossing fast spots and a place to lean if you get tired in the middle of a crossing. Needing a break can be a real issue because wading fast water gives your entire body a great cardiovascular workout, and even people who are otherwise strong and adept at sports use muscles they don't ordinarily exercise, so a rest in the middle of the river can make a huge difference.

Staffs come in all different styles, from expandable aluminum or graphite models that fit into a little waist pouch to full-length wooden models. Some have rubber tips, and some have metal tips. Metal tips are better in really slippery conditions, but they are also noisy and may frighten spooky fish by sending strong vibrations through the water. Rubber tips are quieter but not quite as secure. Some models offer interchangeable tips that you can switch depending on conditions. All wading staffs should include a lanyard that attaches to your wading belt. It allows you to just drop the staff when you get into position to fish without worrying about losing it, but even more important is the ability to retrieve your staff if you lose your grip in the middle of a crossing.

You don't have to buy fancy wading staffs for everyone. Ski poles or hiking staffs work in a pinch, and you can make a nice staff out of a long broom or shovel handle or a piece of heavy-duty hardwood dowel. Just make sure you attach some kind of lanyard. And in a pinch, a stout branch scrounged from the shoreline will work for the occasional difficult crossing. Just make sure you test the branch before you start across the river. Lean on it in several directions with all your weight to make sure it does not have a weak spot that you didn't notice. I use these natural staffs all the time, and once I cross the river in a good spot, I leave the stick in a place I'll notice so that I can cross at the same spot when I return. If you make your own staff, make sure that it reaches to the shoulder of the person using it, because it will be used in the water and needs to be long enough to reach into the edge of a deep pocket.

A wading staff is essential when fishing fast current. This one collapses into a handy pouch that hangs from your wading belt.
COURTESY ORVIS

PFDs Are Not a Bad Idea

If anyone in your family is a poor swimmer or unsure on their feet, a personal flotation device is a good idea. The permanently buoyant vests worn by kayakers are far less bulky and hot than PFDs of the past, and you can even find ones with pockets that can hold small amounts of fishing gear so they can be worn in place of a fishing vest. For small children who may not be strong swimmers, I'd invest in the type that has a collar in back, which not only helps keep them face up if they fall in, but also offers protection against banging the back of their head on rocks in strong current.

Another less bulky option is the inflatable PFD, which operates by inflating a buoyant collar with CO_2 from a gas cartridge. Most of these have the option of being manually triggered with a ripcord-type device, but some models have an automatic feature that inflates the vest automatically if it is submerged.

What to Do if You Fall In

If you wade enough, you'll fall in eventually, and so will members of your family. Usually it involves a bit of sputtering, a few laughs, and perhaps the demise of an unprotected cell phone. In forty-five years of fly fishing, I have never fallen in where I couldn't immediately get up and walk to shore after swimming just a few strokes, so I don't want to scare you into keeping your whole family off the water, but people do drown while wading. Like CPR, a flotation device is something you will probably never use, but that one time in your life when you need it, it can mean the difference between life and death.

The usual advice if you fall in fast water and get carried away is to get your feet downstream to fend off rocks. This can be dangerous when wearing waders, though, because even with a wading belt, you present a wide profile to the current with open waders facing into the current, preventing you from swimming to shore. I think it's better to immediately swim as hard as possible to the shallows while keeping an eye out for rocks ahead, fending them off if needed with your arms. Keeping your face sideways to waves also prevents you from gulping in a mouthful of water if a standing wave hits you full force.

Kids should always wear a PFD in a boat. Modern ones are very comfortable and not bulky.

If you see a tree or log lying in the water ahead, swim around it if you can. Trees lying in the water, known as "sweepers," probably account for more drownings in rivers than any other kind of structure because a strong current can pin you up against a log or even under it, making self-rescue or even rescue efforts by others almost impossible. If you can't avoid a sweeper, swim as hard as possible toward it, and at the last minute launch your body upward while kicking as hard as you can, then try to crawl up onto the log. Do everything you can to avoid getting your feet under a sweeper, because once they get trapped in the hydraulics below, there is very little chance you'll be able to get them out.

Instead, aim for gravel bars or riffles when floating downstream. Avoid areas of smooth or swirly water, which are probably deeper than the rest of the river. If your waders have filled with water, once you get to the shallows you may not be able to stand up, so you should crawl to shore or remove your waders. Then get into dry clothes or a warm car as soon as possible, or get a fire started in a hurry, to prevent hypothermia.

Saltwater Wading

Wading in salt water presents special challenges because not only is the current often as strong as it is in swift trout streams, but the current direction and depth can change quickly due to tidal action. Luckily wading in salt water is often done without waders, so swimming is easier if you run into problems, but not always. When wading the redfish flats in Florida in February, or the surf in the Northeast all summer long, waders are often worn because of cold water. So the same safety rules apply—especially the precaution of wearing a wading belt.

Tidal currents can be deceiving because the bottom of tidal flats is often uneven, with higher points of land like sandbars and oyster bars forming far offshore. Tides can rush in behind you, making it impossible to get back to shore. When wading out onto tidal flats, always begin wading with a falling tide and remember the deep spots on your way out. And as soon as the tide begins to turn, start heading back to shore—don't wait until it is too late. Fog can also roll in quickly with the turn of the tide, particularly in the Northeast. A compass and/or GPS are essential

Wading for saltwater species is not just for tropical waters. Striped bass and bluefish in the Northeast are often caught by wading anglers.

when wading anyplace that fog is even possible. If you are relying solely on GPS, make sure the unit is waterproof and has fresh batteries.

Wading fishermen drown on a regular basis on the gentle flats of Cape Cod Bay, where you can wade up to a mile offshore on a falling tide. Typically this happens because the fishing is good as far out as you can wade, and when the tide rolls in the fishing gets even better, so anglers stay out too long. Fog and deep channels with strong current inshore of the low-tide line often play a part as well. If you wade out into salt water with your family, stay within sight and yelling distance of each other and make sure at least one of you has a compass or GPS.

Boat Safety

Standard boat safety should apply when you fish with your family, and it's wise to be even more vigilant than when you are out for a simple boat ride because fishing, especially fly fishing, distracts boaters. Kids should always wear a PFD, as should all adults who are not strong swimmers. When fishing with one or more of your family, consider a rowboat or wide-beamed canoe. Even with very stable craft, pay attention when someone lands a fish, as there is a natural tendency for everyone to lean over the same side to look at the fish, increasing the danger of capsizing.

If you plan on floating a river without an experienced guide, make sure that everyone in your family is briefed beforehand on river safety by a guide. Know what kind of water is around every bend, stay together if you have multiple boats, and if the river in question is higher than normal, stay out of boats altogether. In the summer of 2011, a number of fly fishers drowned because water levels were higher than normal, and even the experienced river guides were caught off guard because currents and obstructions had changed with spring floods. And even gentle flows can pin a boat up against a submerged tree, making escape or rescue impossible.

Never take your family on a river trip with float tubes or belly boats. It's very difficult to get out of one of these if you get into trouble, and because they are not made to negotiate currents, it's even difficult to avoid obstructions, much less extricate yourself. Inflatable pontoon boats, with oars or paddle fins, are safer because if the craft tips over you can get out of it easily, as you are not strapped in as you are with a float tube.

When fishing with guides, first make sure the river you are about to float is not in flood or rising because of hydroelectric releases. If it is, think twice about taking that float. I'd also be wary of any river guide that does not give you a safety talk before you get into a boat. The good ones tell you where all the life jackets are located if you don't plan to wear them, how the anchor works, and how to maneuver the boat and avoid obstructions in case one of you has to handle the boat while the guide attempts a rescue or is otherwise indisposed. And once the float starts, pay attention to the water coming up and listen for directions from the guide. If you're standing in the bow casting and he tells you to sit down, listen to him and immediately get your butt on the seat. He may have spotted a new log in the river or the water may have dropped, exposing rocks that can jar the boat and eject you if you're not prepared.

Lightning

Although they look like plastic, graphite rods conduct electricity very well. Lightning can strike miles from a storm center, especially in the arid western United States, so if lightning is seen or thunder is heard, get that 9-foot lightning rod out of your hands quickly. Golfers aren't the only people who get killed by lightning. If a storm catches you off guard and your rod starts to vibrate or you get static shocks from it, put the rod down and get to a low spot away from high trees. If you have to walk to get to safety, break your rod down and carry it low. Fishing isn't very good in the middle of a thunderstorm anyway, as it puts the fish off.

Sun

No one needs to be reminded of the dangers of ultraviolet rays to exposed skin and eyes. The one special consideration when fishing is that when you are in and around water, you get almost a double dose of sun because of reflection. Wear strong sunscreen and a long-sleeved shirt and long pants wherever possible, and don't scrimp on sunglasses. Good sunglasses block 100 percent of UVA and UVB rays and will be marked as such, and they will also block much of the infrared (IR) radiation, which in the short term makes eyes dry and tired, so it is especially important to block IR radiation if you have a long drive home after your fishing trip.

Hooks

Hooks today are razor sharp, and it's said that during a cast the hook travels through the air at over 100 miles per hour. A hook in the arm is a minor annoyance that can be removed easily, followed by a tetanus booster if needed. A hook in the eye can be life-changing, and people have been blinded while fly fishing. Even experienced casters hook themselves when a rogue gust of wind sweeps the cast across their body.

First and foremost is eye and head protection. Hats with wide brims and flaps in the back keep flies away from your neck and face. Sunglasses with wraparound lenses keep flies away from the eyes. Kids especially like to experiment with their casting and are not always as aware of the proximity of other people, but in the excitement of heavy fish-feeding activity, anyone can get distracted, so everyone in your family, whether they are actually fishing or just watching, should always wear a hat and sunglasses, even on days when the sun is not shining. And if fishing into the dark, take along a pair of clear safety glasses.

Flies are easy to remove from skin, except near or in the eye. If a fly buries itself in an eye or near one, cut the tippet and immediately get the affected person to a hospital. There is really nothing else you can do. If the fly penetrates anywhere else, first hope it's a barbless fly, in which case it can be quickly backed out without any special procedure. Clean the wound as you would any other puncture, and get a tetanus booster if you need one.

Barbed flies are also surprisingly easy to remove, and I am always amazed when I meet a fly fisher who does not know this trick, but many don't. First, get a strong piece of monofilament, either the heavier end of your leader or tippet that measures at least 10 pounds (2X works great). Loop the monofilament over the bend of the hook and wrap the open ends around one finger so they are very secure. Next, press down as hard as you can on the eye of the hook and jerk the monofilament loop. The hook will pop out cleanly every time, even barbed hooks, with very little tissue damage.

It's a good idea to tell the person you are working on that you will pull out the hook on a count of three, and then pop it out after you count to one. That way they don't flinch and the hook will be out before they even realize what's happened. I've used this technique on myself numerous times when no one else was around, and I remember one day on the upper Connecticut River in northern Vermont when I must have been particularly clumsy, as I had to use this procedure on myself three times in one afternoon!

Ouch! A hook in the arm is no fun but easy to remove.

Slip a length of tippet material around the bend of the hook and firmly press down on the eye.

By jerking the tippet quickly, even a barbed hook pops out with almost no tissue damage.

Chapter 10

Family Fly Fishing and Conservation

There is a common perception that fly fishing is somehow more contemplative than other types of fishing, and that people who fly fish are more in tune with the environment and thus stronger conservationists. I think I'd argue with the contemplative aspect, as I can't think of anything more contemplative than sitting on the bank of a lake or river fishing with a worm, waiting for something to happen. Fly fishing may actually be the least contemplative kind of fishing because it involves us physically and mentally. I know that many times while fly fishing I've completely ignored spectacular scenery and have even been totally oblivious to the presence of a bear on the far bank, not 50 feet away.

But I would argue that fly fishers are in a better position to be strong conservationists. In order to be successful at fly fishing, we have to pay attention to the prey that fish eat, and thus we're more in tune with food webs and how various kinds of plants and animals are interconnected and how they depend on each other. And with many kinds of fly fishing, we need to get closer to the fish and observe them as they feed, so we have a better idea of how a fish interacts with its environment than someone who fires as many casts as possible per minute with a spinning lure or who sits in a boat with bait hanging in deep water, waiting for a fish to swim along.

Fly fishing is a perfect way to get your family in tune with the natural world. Turning over rocks in a stream helps us figure out what kinds of larvae trout may eat and thus what pattern of nymph to use, but it also brings us back to our childhood, and when we do this with our kids, it puts us all on the same level of interest. Watching a bass eat a frog or a pike eat a mouse not only tells us what fly pattern to try, it also helps us show our kids that having a healthy population of fish for our sport depends on the reproductive success of mice and the protection of amphibians from acid rain and pesticides.

I think that many parents and people who teach other adults about fly fishing stress the importance of releasing fish and believe that because they practice catch-and-release, they are doing their job as conservationists. This is a misguided approach. First, there is nothing morally wrong about killing fish and eating them. I would argue that a special dinner of brook trout taken from a small mountain stream allows us to celebrate and respect the fish more, and helps to show our children where their food comes from.

Releasing fish we catch does not protect fish populations for future generations, as I have heard many people say. It only stockpiles fish for the current generation. I won't argue that releasing most of the fish we catch makes fishing better for everyone in the short term because more fish are left in a stream or lake, but fisheries scientists have proven time and again that fish populations are seldom limited by the number of spawning pairs of fish in a given lake or stream. When there are many spawners and thus many young fish, more predators are attracted and there are fewer safe habitats available to each fish, so the survival rate is lower. When there are few spawning pairs of fish, those fish that hatch have more food and more available cover for protection, and fewer predators are attracted, so survival is higher and the stream is able to reach its carrying capacity within a few generations. It is very difficult to "fish out" a lake or stream as long as there is suitable spawning habitat and protective habitat for fish once they hatch.

In our busy lives, few of us have the time, money, and energy to contribute to the conservation arena on many fronts. Thus it's far more important to teach our children and fishing partners that *habitat* is the most important part of the environment to maintain and protect, and to understand what constitutes important habitat requires an understanding of the needs not only of the species we fish for, but also those critters they need to eat in order to survive.

Habitat Protection

There are few things a family can do on its own to protect habitat. Ensuring that a trout stream stays cold enough to support populations of wild trout can depend on land use practices throughout the watershed, impoundments on the stream, drainage from roads and parking lots, and even the pace of global warming. These are issues that depend on the right laws being written, proper enforcement of regulations, and the education of all users of the water. Those issues depend on forming groups of people who can speak with a powerful single voice. A group can hire scientists to prove the efficacy of habitat protection, or even economists who can show the economic benefit of sport fishing in a healthy stream as opposed to a shopping mall that might threaten a stream or lake by replacing native vegetation with asphalt and concrete, which increases siltation and raises water temperatures. Equally important is the ability of these groups to speak loudly enough to grab the attention of lawmakers wishing to be reelected.

Even in our vast oceans, where some threats do come from excessive fishing pressure, habitat protection may be just as critical. Tarpon, snook, and redfish are well protected from overfishing with strict catch limits, but these fish depend entirely on inland brackish water mangrove swamps for spawning and juvenile habitat. One family would have trouble preventing a housing development from draining a valuable mangrove swamp, but hundreds or even thousands of families speaking with one voice can make a difference.

My suggestion is to pick the one conservation organization that does the most to protect the habitats you care about most, and have the whole family not only join the organization but stay active in it. Many have family memberships, and some, like Trout Unlimited, have special membership categories for kids, where they get their own newsletter on cold-

Allowing sheep to graze right down to the riverbanks caused this massive erosion and a loss of valuable pasture. A small buffer strip of vegetation along the banks would have saved both the pasture and the river.

water conservation topics, with articles, puzzles, and games that teach conservation basics.

Sometimes habitat work is on a small scale, such as shoring up an eroding bank that adds to siltation in a stream, or planting trees to provide bank stabilization and lower water temperatures by providing shade. Sometimes cattle need to be fenced in to keep them from eroding unstable banks, and many family farms don't have the additional resources to fence large tracts of riparian habitat. Organizations like Trout Unlimited or American Rivers often support projects to manage these smaller habitat issues by obtaining the required permits and then providing funds, materials, and strong backs to complete the work. Most of the labor is from volunteers, and I can't think of a better way to teach your family about conservation and instill a strong conservation ethic than getting together for an afternoon of rolling rocks around in the mud or planting trees to protect habitat.

Organizations to Join

There are hundreds of local and national conservation organizations, and they all have their place. The following conservation organizations are the ones most fly fishers support, largely because of the work they do in fisheries that fly fishers care about most.

Trout Unlimited

1300 North 17th St., Ste. 500
Arlington, VA 22209-2404
(703) 522-0200 or (800) 834-2419
www.tu.org

Trout Unlimited is the strongest and most organized of cold-water (trout, steelhead, and salmon) habitat protection organizations, with a strong national office, a large full-time staff of fisheries scientists, and both state and local volunteer chapters. They tackle projects from planting trees on small streams to stopping the construction of dams where they are environmentally unfeasible.

American Rivers

1101 14th St. NW, Ste. 1400
Washington, DC 20005
(202) 347-7550
www.americanrivers.org

American Rivers is not just a fishing organization—its members include boaters and naturalists as well. But it does important work through its five areas of concentration: rivers and global warming, river restoration, river protection, clean water, and water supply.

The Federation of Fly Fishers

5237 US 89 South, Ste. 11
Livingston, MT 59047
(406) 222-9369
www.fedflyfishers.org

In addition to its conservation work, the Federation of Fly Fishers also supports education and the ethics of fly fishing. Its many local chapters often have strong conservation programs, and the national organization includes conservation as one of its major areas of focus.

Coastal Conservation Association
6919 Portwest, Ste. 100
Houston, TX 77024
(713) 626-4234 or (800) 201-FISH
www.joinCCA.org
The stated purpose of the Coastal Conservation Association is to advise and educate the public on conservation of marine resources. Its objective is to conserve, promote, and enhance the present and future availability of these coastal resources for the benefit and enjoyment of the general public. The organization works mainly through various state chapters. It has chapters in most states along the Atlantic and Gulf coasts, as well as Oregon and Washington on the West Coast.

Bonefish & Tarpon Trust
24 Dockside Lane, PMB 83
Key Largo, FL 33037
(239) 283-4733
www.tarbone.org
The Bonefish & Tarpon Trust focuses mainly on research, because at this point we don't know much about the life cycle and reproductive needs of ocean species, and without that knowledge we can't work to protect critical habitats. Besides bonefish and tarpon, the organization also studies and works to protect redfish, snook, and permit, which often utilize the same habitat as bonefish and tarpon.

Invasive Species

Invasive species of many different kinds of plants and animals pose a serious threat to the health of our aquatic ecosystems. Once introduced to new habitat, these life forms often find unexploited niches with no natural predators to keep them in check, and their populations explode

Didymo, also known as rock snot, is an alga that has become a nuisance in some rivers. It's likely that one cause of the spread of this invasive species was anglers' wading gear that was not properly cleaned, dried, and inspected.

at the expense of native species. To cite just a couple of examples: Zebra mussels are small mollusks that strain algae from freshwater, removing algae and its primary productivity from an ecosystem. Because no native species eat zebra mussels, this productivity is lost from the system. Didymo is a filamentous alga native to northeastern North America. When transported to places like the Rocky Mountains or New Zealand, it can grow unchecked and clog rivers with a plant that native species are unable to eat.

Parasites are another issue. Whirling disease is caused by a protozoan parasite carried by an aquatic worm that originated in Europe, where native brown trout evolved resistance. But when the parasite was introduced into the United States via infected hatchery fish, it ran wild in populations of wild rainbow trout. The parasite attacks the nervous system of young fish, crippling their spine and making them swim in circles, giving the disease its name.

Although rubber-soled wading boots with studs (left) dry quicker than felt soles, they still hold mud and other debris and should be scrubbed with a wire brush before moving to another watershed to prevent the spread of the spores and eggs of invasive species.

Although not all invasive species were introduced by fishermen, many of them (and their eggs or spores) can be transported by anglers via water and algae left in boats or by surviving in their wading gear. Felt soles on wading boots, because they offer many tiny crevices and dry very slowly, were found to be able to transport many of these organisms. This is why felt soles are gradually being banned by state and regional laws.

Fishermen are not totally responsible for the spread of these destructive exotics, and in most cases were probably not the major factor. Stocking of diseased hatchery fish originally distributed whirling disease, but it is suspected that felt soles carried whirling disease spores to many other waters (the spores are incredibly resistant to freezing and drying). There is compelling evidence that fishermen were also the initial vector for didymo. Of course, ducks, geese, mergansers, herons, otters, and beavers are also responsible for moving aquatic invasives around. But otters don't hop on a plane and fly to New Zealand, and ducks seldom migrate east and west.

So as anglers who wade in streams, you and your family should do everything in your power to help prevent the spread not only of these invasive species but also of diseases and harmful organisms we don't even know about yet. Just replacing felt soles with studded rubber soles is not the whole answer. Rubber soles can still hold mud and debris and transport it from one place to another, but rubber dries quicker, which kills some invasives, and is easier to clean, which removes all of them.

When your family moves from one watershed to another, clean your boat by washing it out, rinsing it completely, and letting it dry before placing it in a new watershed. Everyone's waders and wading shoes should be washed in hot water and soap, cleaned thoroughly with a wire brush, and then allowed to dry completely before putting them in new watersheds. Adhering to this practice on a regular basis not only will help control the spread of invasives but will also educate your family on the danger of introducing alien species to nonnative watersheds.

Because the laws on felt soles and the dangers of new aquatic invasive species are constantly being updated, you and your family can keep on top of the issue by visiting the Clean Angler website at www.clean angling.org and by asking everyone in the family to take the Clean Angling Pledge, which simply states: "I pledge to inspect, clean, and dry my gear after every use."

Family Conservation Activities

Besides practicing clean-angling rules and joining a conservation organization and getting involved with its projects, there are a few things your family can do on its own to help preserve and maintain aquatic habitats.

Planting Trees

Trees along shorelines stabilize the banks with their root systems and provide shade that lowers water temperatures, mitigating increases in temperature due to development, road building, poor grazing practices,

Planting willow shoots along eroded banks is a great family activity and benefits all kinds of wildlife.

and global warming. By stabilizing riverbanks, their root systems prevent erosion and silt, which is beneficial because silt fills in pools, resulting in loss of fish habitat and even loss of property. When pools fill up with silt, floods push river water into the surrounding land and can destroy roads and houses. Silt also smothers fish eggs, young fish, and aquatic insect larvae.

When trees fall in the water after they die, they provide protection for both adult and young fish. In fact, the presence of woody debris has a strong correlation to the density of a fish population and has been proven to be even more important than food supply in determining the health of trout streams. (Food is seldom a limiting factor in trout streams, as there is always more food drifting in the current than trout can utilize.)

I can't think of a single reason not to encourage the growth of trees along any river (except that they tend to make us lose flies on our back-casts!). You and your family can actually encourage the growth of trees along your favorite stream, and what a great feeling it is to plant some willow shoots as a family and return year after year to see the bank stabilizing and getting healthier.

Sometimes young trees are available through Trout Unlimited chapters or local conservation districts, and they always provide volunteers to help plant them. But you can even do this on your own. If you identify an eroding bank while fishing in the spring, you and your family can cut young saplings and shoots while they are just beginning to form buds and then simply stick these into the bank, or dig up young saplings and plant them in a shallow hole, just as you would in your yard.

The best trees or shrubs to plant are those that already occur along the banks, because you know those will take root. Trees and shrubs like willow, alder, and red osier dogwood are common along streams and will take root easily. Plant them in damp ground, but not too close to the bank or floods may wash them away. The benefits the river will obtain from roots can come from trees many yards away. It helps to tie bigger saplings to a stake, and if beavers are common and you have the resources, wire guards around the trunks will keep them from being eaten. Once the trees take root, though, being chewed by beavers is not so bad because the natural reaction of a tree like a willow—if the main shoot is eaten—is to spread out its root system, further stabilizing the ground.

Not all the trees you plant will take, and if the stream bank suffers a destructive flood, none of them may survive. But by making this a family project, you can stress the importance of riparian vegetation to everyone and help them look at the stream environment in a different way.

Landowner Relations

Typically landowners along rivers are the main drivers for how the habitat is maintained or degraded. Second-home owners cut all the trees along a riverbank so they have a nice view. Ranchers find it easier to let their livestock drink from the river any place they want and trample its banks rather than fence them in and just allow them access to water at specific points. Most landowners don't take kindly to government officials or Trout Unlimited members telling them what to do with their land—especially ranchers and dairy farmers.

But often these same people don't realize they'd lose less of their valuable property by maintaining the banks, or that the erosion on their property is filling in pools far downstream and flooding the basements of people who live along the river many miles away. In my experience, farmers don't often fish because their life is too busy to spend time fishing for recreation, but I have also found that they enjoy seeing someone else getting pleasure out of the use of their river, especially when it involves an entire family.

Getting someone to change their land-use pattern is a long and delicate process. You can't walk up to landowners and tell them they're ruining your fishing because they cut their lawn all the way down to the river or their cattle are destroying the banks. The first thing to do is to ask permission to fish on their property, even if the land is not posted as private. You cannot believe how much trust and respect that garners, particularly with farmers. The next step is to check in with them every time you fish, even if they tell you, "No problem, you can fish there any time." Take your spouse and kids. Ask to look at the new calves in the barn. Learn about their way of life.

This process may take a year or more, but once you have gained their trust, ask if you can help stop the erosion on their banks by getting a bunch of friends together, buying some fence posts, and renting a post-hole digger, or just ask if they mind if you plant a few trees along the bank. Let them know you think a few more trees along the bank or keeping the cattle out of the river will make a healthier river system both for them and for your kids to enjoy in the future. It won't always work and it won't work with everyone, but at the very least you will have educated not only your family but also the landowner on good land-use practices.

I've been involved in many stream improvement projects over the years, as a volunteer, landowner, neighbor, and board member of a local conservation alliance. It's seldom the money or the permits that determine how much work gets done on a stream. The hardest part of the process is getting landowner permission and cooperation, and anything you and your family can do to help this process will benefit the ecosystem.

Afterword

At the beginning of this book, I lied to you. I implied that fly fishing was no more complex than other kinds of fishing, and that it was not very expensive and was easy to learn. But the other side of the coin is that once fly fishing takes hold of your life, you live and breathe it twelve months a year, whether you are able to get to water or not. You spend more money on tackle. You save your extra money for a trip to Alaska. You even fantasize about getting a job in the fly-fishing business. (Take my advice—don't. It's a tiny industry with low-paying jobs and few positions available. Keep your day job so you can make enough money to support your addiction.)

You can keep fly fishing simple and inexpensive, but the reality is that most of us don't. We love the complexity. We enjoy buying gear. We begin to realize that if we fly fish for the rest of our lives, we'll be learning new secrets up to the last time we go fly fishing, so we never really master it. If your family enjoys fly fishing with the same passion you do, it can be an amazing bond. But be prepared for something less than your dream. If you can at least enjoy a few fly-fishing trips a year with your family, and if they have an appreciation of your passion, that's all most of us can expect. And if you get that far, you'll be ahead of most fly-fishing fanatics in the world today.

Acknowledgments

Not all books are fun to write, but this one was. It was fascinating to hear detailed stories of how all different kinds of families learned to enjoy fly fishing together, and also encouraging that most everything I learned was consistent despite differences in age, family dynamics, or prior fishing experience. For sharing their experiences in detail, I'd like to thank Tyler Adkins, Colin Archer, Shawn Comar, Jane Cooke, Ronan Cooke, Bob Eastway, Teresa Eastway, Evan Griggs, Don Haynes, Norma Haynes, Jon Luke, Sam Mosheim, Caleb Parent, Dan Parent, Chrissy Penn, Rich Seminek, Dean Wormell, and Valerie Wormell.

I would like to thank Greg Burchstead and Justin Coleman for helping me understand the psychological benefits of fly fishing to families. Justin references two studies, and they are as follows:

Beets, M. W., R. Vogel, S. Chapman, K. H. Pitetti, and B. J. Cardinal. 2007. "Parent's social support for children's outdoor physical activity: Do weekdays and weekends matter?" *Sex Roles* 56(1): 125–31.

Bois, J. E., P. G. Sarrazin, R. J. Brustad, D. O. Trouilloud, and F. Cury. 2005. "Elementary schoolchildren's perceived competence and physical activity involvement: The influence of parents' role modelling behaviours and perceptions of their child's competence." *Psychology of Sport and Exercise* 6(4): 381–97.

Guides are the heroes and true experts of the fly-fishing world. They deal with all kinds of families and individuals every day and almost always make a fun and rewarding experience out of it. The following guides in particular were especially helpful in sharing their secrets for making guide trips and lodge experiences special times for families: Jim Hickey, John Packer, Simon Perkins, and Rick Ruoff. Molly Seminek is both a guide and an expert on teaching women how to fly fish (she's actually one of the finest teachers I've ever seen, period, but she specializes in teaching women), and I am fortunate to have the benefit of her wisdom. Melanie, Patrick Jr., and Patrick Sr. Timmins of Rawah

Ranch were especially helpful in showing me how to make a ranch family friendly, even with a cranky six-year-old.

Thanks to Eric Weisledder and Tim Bronson for helping me photograph the fly stuck in my arm.

Tucker Bamford, Rob Ceccarini, George Layton, Rich Merlino, and Leland Miyawaki, all fishing managers of Orvis stores, took time out of their very busy days to point out the excellent urban fisheries in some of our biggest metropolitan areas.

And finally, many thanks to my kids, Brooke and Brett, and my wife, Robin, for letting me use them as guinea pigs for some of my teaching experiments. Only time will tell if it will stick or not, but it's been a fun journey so far.

Index

About the Author

Tom Rosenbauer, host of the Orvis Fly Fishing Podcasts, has been with the Orvis Company for over thirty years, and while there has been a fishing school instructor, copywriter, public relations director, and merchandise manager, along with editor of the *Orvis News* for ten years. He has fished extensively across North America and has also fished on Christmas Island, the Bahamas, in Kamchatka, and on the fabled English chalk streams. He is credited with bringing bead-head flies to North America and is the inventor of the Big Eye hook, Magnetic Net Retriever, and tungsten beads for fly tying.

He has ten fly-fishing books in print. He has also been published in *Field & Stream, Outdoor Life, Catalog Age, Fly Fisherman, Gray's Sporting Journal, Sporting Classics, Fly Rod & Reel, Audubon,* and other magazines. He lives in southern Vermont on the banks of his favorite trout stream.

Tom is *Fly Rod & Reel* magazine's 2011 Angler of the Year. To quote the magazine: "People who meet him know this: Rosenbauer is as valid a fly fisherman as they come—honest, approachable, generous, dedicated, and enthusiastic. It's that kind of enthusiasm and the written and verbal legacy he is providing that make Tom Rosenbauer *Fly Rod & Reel's* 2011 Angler of the Year."